Randori-no-kata

JORMA PAASI

JUDO

RANDORI-NO-KATA

NAGE-NO-KATA · KATAME-NO-KATA

乱取りの形

投の形・固の形

Copyright 2023 and 2024; text @JORMA PAASI; drawings @JORMA PAASI;
Publisher:BoD · Books on Demand, Mannerheimintie 12 B, 00100 Helsinki,
bod@bod.fi
Printed by: Libri Plureos GmbH, Friedensallee 273, 22763 Hamburg, Germany

Photographs @JORMA PAASI and PETER MICKELSSON
Graphic design JUKKA AALTO · ARMADILLO GRAPHICS
Layout JORMA PAASI
ISBN: 978-952-80-9523-1

Dedicated to Päivi and seven others

TABLE OF CONTENTS

FOR THE READER

This book describes nage-no-kata and katame-no-kata. They are collectively called randori-no-kata, because the skills presented by both kata are needed in free practice.

Writing a kata book is not quite straightforward. Although katas have remained the same for a long time, different emphasis has been placed on different things at different times. One should be able to describe the essentials but avoid introducing the last superficial details, strong opinions or preferences as the truth. I have tried to present the kata as they are defined by the IJF (International Judo Federation) and Kodokan at the time of writing the book.

In many countries, judokas are introduced to kata for the first time in the blue belt grading examination and it means learning the nage-no-kata and its first three throws. But this is only a glimpse of what judo katas contain. The number of techniques in the official kata of Kodokan is close to 130. This book covers 30 of them.

Why are kata still required to be presented in grading examination? This question is appropriate if judo is to be understood as a purely competitive sport among other sports. But judo is also much more than that. It has a deeper and broader history and foundation than many other sports. Some of this is only revealed by examining the kata. It is often not seen that the randori and kata are two different sides of judo. They both help to understand a better and more holistic understanding of judo.

When studying the kata, one can only be amazed at how systematically techniques have been studied and taught in jujutsu schools for a long time before the birth of judo. A method that has been used in judo for almost 140 years, kata, can provide many judoka with a good tool for the development of their own judo. At the same time, kata works both as a teaching method and a learning tool.

There are several steps in learning kata. First, you learn by imitation to perform the correct kind of performance according to the teacher's model. Learning the movements, but not the content. The next stage is to better understand why something is done the way it is done. You start to get inside the kata. In the next stage, you already understand the basics, which allows you to start making your own kata. Movements are best done with a technique suited to your own and your partner's physical abilities. At the highest level, kata becomes almost automatic. Actions are made according to the situation. At this level, it does not matter if uke attacks with the wrong technique. For each situation, tori chooses the right technique.

The best way to learn kata is on the tatami with a competent teacher. There must also be other sources to support learning. Videos show for the beginner the visible part and the external shell of kata. A book gives an opportunity to describe the actions of tori and uke more accurately. The text and images can draw the reader's attention to the critical points that matter. The reader can freely explore the techniques and form his own understanding of the correct performance. After reading the book, the reader can discover new dimensions in the techniques also from videos.

The purpose of the book is to serve as a guide and to help nage-no-kata and katame-no-kata learning. The book first introduces the common features of both kata, then the general features of the kata in question, followed by a detailed description of each technique. Among these, it also presents the principles and lessons that the techniques contain.

The reason I have highlighted the previous practices is that the perception of kata has changed a lot over the last twenty years. In many kata books there are details that are no longer taught today. I have wanted to emphasise this change and the fact that the concept of the right and wrong depends on the principles that are desired to be emphasized at any given time.

Each kata master has his/her own way of doing kata. Flavours are different, but the principles presented in the kata should still remain the same.

SPELLING AND NOTATION

For the spelling of Japanese words, I have followed the convention of separating words with a hyphen, as in harai-goshi. For the names of the kata, I have chosen the form nage-no-kata, because Kodokan uses it on its website and in its textbooks of different kata. I also find it more easy to read. I also use the commonly used forms Kodokan, judo, Jigoro Kano and o-soto-gari, although the more accurate spelling is Kōdōkan, jūdō, Jigorō Kanō and ō-soto-gari. When I have wanted to highlight the Japanese pronunciation or the difference in meaning of similar words, I use the macron (long character). For example, go is different from gō. The first is five and the second is hard.

At the beginning of each technique, the principle, teaching, kuzushi (only in nage-no-kata) and important points.

The starting and the ending positions of each technique are illustrated with drawings, and Tori is shown with darker hair. Regarding the ukemi, the area where uke should end up after the throw is shown roughly. In katame-no-kata the movement of tori is shown prior to the initial situation.

! An exclamation mark indicates the text with additional details of the technique.

* An asterisk indicates text with training tips or escapes in katame-no-kata.

The movement directions are always referred to in relation to shomen (place of honoured guests). That which is to the right in the photograph taken from the direction of the shomen, is also on the right in the text. For example, 'tori is on the right and uke on the left'.

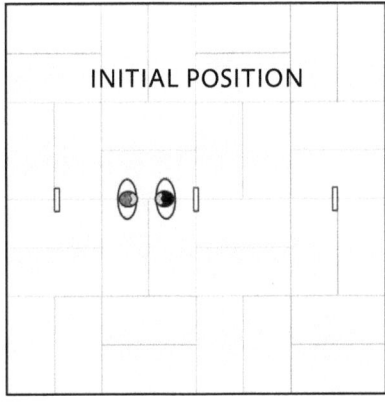

INITIAL POSITION

SHOMEN

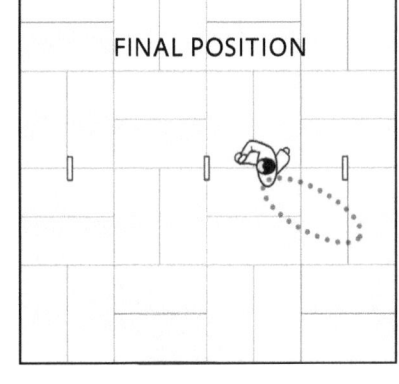

FINAL POSITION

SHOMEN

JUDO KATAS AND THEIR EVOLUTION

HISTORY OF KATA IN GENERAL

The Japanese word kata (形) means form, pattern or even standard. It can mean both singular and plural. It can be said that there is one nage-no-kata or nage-no-kata contains 15 kata. Kata as a concept is not limited to martial arts of Japanese origin, but for example, the tea ceremony is also a kind of kata.

In Japan, kata were the means by which the samurai's skills were transferred from one generation to the next. In jujutsu schools, the focus was on close combat skills, and they included hundreds of different types of kata, which were taught by the masters to their students. The teachings of different master's, however, were divergent. Additions could be made to them or they could be influenced by other jujutsu schools (ryu). In this case, a new school was established and the new school continued this new doctrine. In this way, new schools were constantly established and by the end of the 19th century there were already hundreds of them. In the same way, Kodokan judo, founded by Jigoro Kano, was born. In the beginning, the name Kodokan judo was used, because in Japan kitō-ryū jujutsu had already in the 18th century used in some contexts, instead of jujutsu, the name judo.

Although many different versions of the different styles of jujutsu have spread, there are few schools that are separated from judo. In Japan, there are some (e.g. Kosen Judo). Brazilian jujutsu can also be counted as a direct descendant of judo. In addition, a few other disciplines, such as the Russian martial art sambo, have taken inspiration from judo. Judo's permanence is largely due to the fact that judo is based not only on different fighting skills, but rather on a broader system created by Kano with a strong philosophical, ethical and educational basis.

When Commodore Perry forced Japan to open its ports in 1854 to the West, Japan established a system of universal conscription army. Initially, military training included, traditional combat skills alongside new weapons. These were taught by many jujutsu schools. The main form of training was kata, but some free practice was also used. Pretty soon it was noted it's not possible to win a modern war with archery or jujitsu skills and their teaching was abolished in 1862. Teaching of all traditional skills (bujutsu) were discontinued in the army in 1866.

The police force continued to teach jujutsu, and it was further developed to make the techniques more suitable for police officers. Old jujutsu schools were having a strong position in this training. To find out the best methods the officials organized matches between jujutsu schools and Kodokan in Tokyo. Judokas succeeded to win these matches, and judo became part of police training.

Samurai, Yokohama, Felis Beato 1864–65.

Dai Nippon Butoku Kai was founded to promote the Japanese martial arts in 1895. Jigoro Kano was elected the president of the jujutsu section, and his task was to standardise the katas for all jujutsu schools in the country. As a result of the work nage-no-kata, kata-me-no-kata and kime-no-kata took their current form.

JUDO TRAINING IN THE EARLY YEARS OF KODOKAN

Jigoro Kano at the age of 30 in 1894. SOURCE: KODOKAN ARCHIVE.

Tenjin shin'yō-ryū technique katajuji-shibori. SOURCE: KODOKAN ARCHIVE.

Jigoro Kano applied to Hachinosuke Fukuda's jujutsu school in 1877. Eleven years earlier, Fukuda had been a teacher in the army. The style of his school was tenjin shin'yō-ryū.

Kano practised both kata and randori at the school. Fukuda died in 1879, after which Masatomo Iso became Kano's teacher. Iso was over 60 years old and taught only kata. Kano's task was to take care of the randori exercises. When Iso died only a few years later, Kano applied to be a student of Tsunetosi Iikubo, whose style was kitō-ryū. Both kata and randori were practiced at that school.

In kitō-ryū, one of the forms of training was kata-nokori or nokori-ai, which was a more informal form of training than kata. This form of training had already been developed in the 18th century, because just learning kata you could not be sure how the technique would work in practice.

The problem was the same as it often is with kata today. Uke may have been too easy to throw or he surrendered too easily. In the kata-nokori tori would take the grip and try a technique that uke would defend against. If tori's technique didn't work, uke was allowed to try a counter-technique. From this situation tori was again allowed to continue. Another method used was to make kata attacks in a random order. Kata-nokori training evolved into a free form of training called randori. Kano further developed randori in Kodokan closer to its current form.

In the very early years of Kodokan, judo training was still taking shape and teaching methods were still evolving. There was no syllabus, no teacher training, and no gokyo-no-waza (five groups of techniques). Later, four main teaching methods took shape: kata, randori, presentation (kōgi) and discussion (mondo). Kata taught the principles, and randori, the application of these principles in reality. Kano considered shiai (competition) to be only one form of randori.

In the beginning, the tenjin shin'yō-ryū and kitō-ryū school kata were used. As the number of trainees increased, Kano realized that he had to develop his own katas for judo. With the new katas, Kano was able to explain and demonstrate the most important principles of judo to a larger number of students. The kata were the first teaching tools of judo. There are no precise descriptions of the contents of the first kata preserved.

Due to his work and long trips abroad, Kano was often absent. The kata enabled Kano to get his closest students to teach precisely the techniques and in the way he wanted. By learning kata students were better and faster able to adopt and utilize the presented principles in the randori.

It was also easier to spread judo to other places when there was a model for doing it. As the number of practitioners began to rise the fundamentals of judo were passed on to new students everywhere in the same form.

Judo training at the Shimotom-izaka Dojo. In the picture, Sakujiro Yokoyama on the left, Kyuzo Mifune on the right, and Jigoro Kano in the background, all wearing dark uniforms. Early 1900s.

SOURCE: KODOKAN ARCHIVE.

DEVELOPMENT OF THE FIRST KATA OF JUDO

The kata developed by Jigoro Kano are nage-no-kata, katame-no-kata, kime-no-kata, ju-no-kata and gō-no-kata. The first one was the nage-no-kata and immediately after that katame-no-kata, both during the period of 1885 and 1886. Gō-no-kata was a kind of opposite of ju-no-kata. It was a kata for the use of force. Kano, however, did not complete the kata, and its practice gradually stopped. Later it has been again restored and demonstrated in public.

The fundamental reason for jujutsu kata was to teach skills to survive in combat. That's why they included some dangerous elements. In developing kata Kano's aim was to eliminate the dangerous elements and concentrate on the optimal use of energy. Each technique chosen for a kata had to represent a principle that Kano wanted to teach. Kodokan teachers needed to understand these principles contained in the kata, and to utilize the principles in randori. In Kano's time it was not possible to reach higher dan grades unless one mastered kata very well.

All the original kata of judo first contained 10 techniques. Later, Kano increased the number of techniques for other kata to 15 and kime-no-kata to 20. Some techniques have since been replaced by others, but most have remained the same.

The choice of techniques and their order was influenced by the fact that the kata had to look harmonious as a whole. For example, the throwing directions had to be in balance with the whole. In addition, the kata had to be a physical exercise and it had to develop the muscle strength and coordination of its practitioner.

Dan-grade awarding ceremony at the Kodokan. Early 1900s.
SOURCE: KODOKAN ARCHIVE.

KODOKAN OFFICIAL KATA   There are nine kata in the official list of Kodokan kata. They include apart from kodomo-no-kata, a total number of 129 techniques.

	KATA	DESCRIPTION	# TECH.
1	NAGE-NO-KATA	Principles of throwing techniques.	15
2	KATAME-NO-KATA	Principles of control techniques on the mat.	15
3	KIME-NO-KATA	An old self-defence kata ("combat kata"), showing defences against attacks with bare hands, knife and sword.	20
4	JU-NO-KATA	A low-paced soft kata with no throws. Ju-no-kata is a physical exercise to increase understanding of the principles of judo.	15
5	KODOKAN GOSHIN-JUTSU	A modern self-defence kata, which involves defending against attacks with bare hands, knife, stick and pistol.	21
6	ITSUTSU-NO-KATA	"The form of five". Contains the main principles of judo in a condensed form. The kata has only five parts.	5
7	KOSHIKI-NO-KATA	Describes situations in armour. A kata of the Kitō-ryū style, modified by Jigoro Kano.	21
8	SEIRYOKU-ZEN'YO-KOKU-MIN-TAIIKU	Contains various physical exercises performed alone and with a partner. This kata also practices strikes and kicks.	8+9
9	KODOMO-NO-KATA	Children's kata, contains many sections with both throws and control techniques.	

Jigoro Kano demonstrating the jigotai stance with Kyuzo Mifune. 1920s or 1930s.

Seiryoku-zen'yo-kokumin-taiiku was created in 1924 and finalized in 1927-28. Kano introduced this kata as an exercise for the physical condition, strikes and kicks. This is the only kata in judo that is partially performed alone.

The modern self-defence kata Kodokan goshin-jutsu was introduced in 1956. The latest addition is the kodomo-no-kata, which was introduced in 2020. It was developed by the Kodokan in collaboration with the IJF and the French Judo Federation. It is a children's kata with elements suitable for different kyu levels.

There are also many unofficial kata. Some of them have been also adopted by the Kodokan, for example the women's self-defence kata joshi goshinhō.

There have been changes in the ceremonies (reiho) of the kata. At the beginning bows were done in shizen-hontai. Until the beginning of World War II za-rei was done like in koshiki-no-kata. Sometimes only ritsu-rei was done. Since then, nage-no-kata and katame-no-kata have an established way of doing za-rei. There was also variation if the left or right knee was put to the mat first. You can also see from old films that it was not so accurate if tori and uke always returned to the same places before the next technique. It was not necessary to adjust the judogi between different wazas.

Jigoro Kano and Yoshitsugu Yamashita. The technique is ko-daore from koshiki-no-kata.
Source: Kodokan archive.

WHAT IS KATA

KATA HAS MANY FORMS   Kata is, among following things:

- Teaching method
- Demonstration tool
- Training method
- Training method for dangerous techniques
- Physical exercise
- Mental exercise
- Test of competence in a grading examination
- Form of competition
- Performance
- Aesthetic entity

Kata is a teaching method that can be used to transfer the model of the correct execution from the teacher to the student. At the same time, information about kuzushi, tsukuri, kake and the right timing of the technique is transferred. Kata is basically a training form that connects judo theory and practice.

Kata is a demonstration tool used to show one or more principles. The technique chosen for nage-no-kata also represents all other throws, which use the same principle. If some throw does not work in practice, it is necessary to investigate which principle related to the throw is missing from the execution. Kata should be practiced to improve judo skills and for the deeper understanding of the essence of judo.

Kata is an exercise method in which, through repetitions, the aim is to achieve automation of execution. Kata practice is done on purpose in a closed form, defined in what needs to be done and how. The formality ensures that tori and uke are both correctly at the right place at the right time. Kata performers can repeat the same execution always the same way. This enables the technique and timing to be honed to perfection, fulfilling the judo principle of "maximum efficiency with minimum effort". Randori training does not give the opportunity to such a simulation because there are so many variables.

Kata is a method of practising techniques that are too dangerous to perform in randori. These are techniques that essentially belong to judo. Especially they exist in kime-no-kata, Kodokan goshin-jutsu and koshi-ki-no-kata.

Kata is a physical exercise. The practice of any kata is a good form of fitness. During a one-hour practice, you can do nage-no-kata in the roles of tori and uke a couple of times. There will be a total of 120 throws. The same number of runs can also be done by focusing on individual throws.

Katame-no-kata is a physically demanding exercise, especially when it comes to osaekomi-waza.

Kata-mawashi from ju-no-kata, performed by Wolfgang Dax-Romswinkel and Ulla Loosen.

Kata is a mental exercise in which you have to live in the moment. During the kata the focus must be solely and exclusively on the kata and its content. If kata is done as a purely mechanical exercise of movements and choreography, without paying attention to its deeper essence, kata becomes a dead imitation exercise.

Kata is a good tool for demonstrating one's technical skills. Nage-no-kata shows the grading committee how well the candidate masters all 15 throwing techniques on both sides. Deficiencies in basic techniques are clearly visible and cannot be compensated for by speed or force. The nage-no-kata is a fair measure to compare different performances to each other. The katame-no-kata is also a good indicator how well the judoka masters escapes and keeps control in changing situations.

Kata is also a form of competition. Kata competitions can be criticized, among other things for deducting points for each error that deviates some defined ideal normal. For the defence of kata competitions it must be said that in order to achieve a very good competition performance a judoka must have been practicing kata for many years. International level kata requires good judo skills, in-depth knowledge of the principles of each technique and how techniques can be made functional in real situations.

Yoko-tsuki from kime-no-kata presented by Marko Ryyppö and Juha Alaluukas.

Kano often used kata in public performances because it was well suited for situations where judo had to be demonstrated. However, he did not mean kata just for performance, and kata was never to be performed only for show.

Ju-no-kata training does not require a tatami, the technique is ago-oshi.

All Kodokan kata are aesthetically pleasing to look at when the kata performers are masterful at what they are doing. In a good kata all its elements and harmony of principles (riai) are clearly visible. The performing couple exudes competence and confidence.

WHAT IS THE RIGHT MODEL? One of the original purposes of the kata was to pass on the model of the right execution from one generation to the next unchanged. The masters taught their students personally and shared their greatest secrets only with their best followers. Some of these, however, may have understood the content of the teachings differently. When these students taught kata further deviations occurred and the way of doing things changed. Originally there may have been small differences in nuance, but after two or three years the kata had already changed into something else.

At one point, the question of uke's role arose in many Western countries. Is uke in nage-no-kata an aggressive attacker or more or less passive in terms of the performance? For example, if uke is the active aggressor then in the techniques where tori moves backwards uke is active and tries to knock tori down. Once tori has retreated enough, tori changes strategy and switches uke's attack to a throw. Interpreted in this way, for example, the uki-otoshi becomes almost a counter-throw. A kata in which uke is aggressive is often identified by its speed. Tori has to quicken his steps to get out of the way. The throws become different and the character of the kata changes.

Different styles of kata have been taught till the early 2000s. The harmonisation of kata teaching started in the early 2010s. The main reason for this was the launch of the kata competitions.

The first step of uki-otoshi, where tori has taken control and uke has already been unbalanced.

Kata competitions were organised in the UK, Germany, Italy and Spain as early as the 1980s. In 1999, the World Master Judo Association (WMJA) organised the first World Cup in Canada. The EJU (European Judo Union) Judo Union) started to organise European championships and judges training in the early 2000s. The IJF became involved in kata competitions in 2008. The katas chosen were nage-no-kata, katame-no-kata, kime-no-kata, ju-no-kata and Kodokan goshin-jutsu. In this context it became necessary to define more precisely what constitutes a good kata and what criteria are used to evaluate kata. The IJF carried out this work in collaboration with Kodokan.

Kodokan also invested heavily in kata education. It organised kata courses around the world and published the English language versions of the main kata textbooks and instructional videos on kata openly available to all.

As a result of the work done, an understanding of all the katas presented at the competitions has become more unified. The aggressive role of uke in the nage-no-kata has been forgotten. In the backward techniques, uke tries to take a grip and initiate an attack, but tori is faster and forces uke to take a longer step than he would have liked. Uke tries to maintain his balance but cannot, because tori won't give him an opportunity to do so.

Although the kata represents a well-defined form, there is still room for interpretation. Kodokan's teachers stress that the kata must be made just naturally. Each kata performer has his or his own style of kata. As long as the style does not violate the principles of kata, deviations are acceptable.

ON EVALUATING KATA The Kodokan kata textbooks and videos and 'Kata competition criteria for evaluation' as defined by the IJF are used as a basis for judging kata. These provide a model that should be followed for both grading examinations as well as in competitions.

In grading examinations the judging methods vary slightly depending on the country and the persons receiving it. Often auxiliary forms are used and the assessment is based on the personal perception of the level of performance. For example, it could be defined that the kata must be more than 50% successful. Failure in a single throw in a nage-no-kata does not mean very much. General uncertainty in all techniques and, for example, the absence of kuzushi means much more. If a

Nordic Judo Kata Open 2022. Uki-otoshi, Tomi-Pekka Takalo tori and Joonas Vakkilainen uke.

technique is completely forgotten and skipped, the examination may be disqualified.

In kata competitions, the start and closing ceremonies and each technique is compared to a perfect ten-point performance, and deviations will be deducted as penalty points. Evaluation of the next technique starts when tori releases his grip after the throw or has moved to the kneeling position (kyoshi) in katame-no-kata.

There are normally five judges. For each technique, the highest and lowest score will be eliminated. The remaining scores will be added to the total score. In smaller competitions three judges will be appointed and the scores of all judges are counted.

The final score is the sum of the scores of each technique. The result will also be expressed as a percentage of the total performance. More than 75 % of the performance is considered to be very good.

THE ROLE OF KATA IN JUDO TRAINING

Kano understood the role of judo in a very broad sense. For him, it was learning fighting skills, developing physical and mental qualities and the pursuit of the common good.

In the early days of Kodokan, kata was taught during randori breaks. Kata was used to show the students the principles in each technique. At the time of the completion of randori-no-kata, the most advanced students of Kano had only been practising judo for a few years. These Kodokan champions to be were still under 25 years old at the time. Kata had been in the centre of the training and the rest of the judo learning took place around it.

Competitors warming up in the main dojo of Kodokan in 2001.

After Kano's death, judo gradually became a sport and success in a competition became the main reason for many judoka to practise judo.

This changed attitudes towards kata, especially in the West. Judokas and coaches who were purely interested in success in competition began to see kata only as a speciality required for grading examinations. At the same time many elements of judo, such as techniques forbidden in competitions, kata, self-defence and atemi (strikes and kicks) were ruled out from training.

It is quite common for a judoka to have been practising for several years before learning any kata. One reason for this late start in kata training is that kata has been seen as a whole rather than as a separate set of individual teaching tools. However, it is worth getting to know the kata on a throw-by-throw basis and only by studying the throwing phase. This is a return to the original purpose of the kata, which was to teach technical purity and correct timing of the throw.

The kata provides an excellent tool for developing technical skills and a holistic understanding of judo for those who wish to practise judo purely for skill development and fitness maintenance. These persons may be new adult practitioners or judoka with age, physical disability or personal preference to whom randori is not meaningful. For the competitive minded persons, kata offers the opportunity to compete up to the highest international levels.

There is no upper age limit for practising judo. Judoka just needs to fit in their own training according to their current fitness and life situation. There is enough to learn in judo and its katas to last a lifetime.

Tsugi-age from ju-no-kata presented by Wolfgang Dax-Romswinkelin and Ulla Loosen.

BASIC CONCEPTS   The basic vocabulary and concepts of judo are also necessary for understanding the kata. Every judoka learns the basic terminology of judo when preparing for a yellow belt grading examination. The words kuzushi, tsukuri and kake become familiar. However, their deeper meaning may need clarification.

KUZUSHI is to unbalance uke and bring him to the position from which the throw can be done. It can be done with hands, body movement or any other way to get uke into a position where he is in danger of losing his balance. Kuzushi can also be done in groundwork judo.

TSUKURI is the preparation of the throw and the positioning of tori for the throw. That is, everything tori does to get himself into the throwing position. Tsukuri may involve pushing, pulling or body movements, waiting for uke's reaction, turning and other movements to optimise tori's throwing position. In some throws, kuzushi precedes the tsukuri and sometimes vice versa.

Kuzushi in katame-no-kata presented by Mikko Tuominen as tori and Samu Laitinen as uke. Kataha-jime.

KAKE is the actual throwing phase.

All kata are further defined by OMOTE and URA. In a kata, the omote is what others see. The ura is the invisible, hidden part of the kata. If a

judoka really wants to get to know the kata, then he must also have to study the ura.

ZANSHIN means the state of alertness after the technique. Tori must be ready to react in case uke continues to attack in any way. This is indicated by a look forward or towards uke, a look of focus without looking anywhere in particular, and by pausing for a moment. Zanshin is used in all types of budo.

Zanshin presented by Marko Ryyppö.
Juha Alaluukas as uke. Tsukkake
from kime-no-kata.

The KATA AREA is the part of the tatami where the kata is performed. It can vary in size. In official competitions it is 8×8 m or 10×10 m. If the edge of the kata area cannot be clearly defined, the first bow should be made either at the edge of the tatami or, for example, around four metres from the centre of the kata area.

The SHOMEN is the place where the recipients of the examination, the guests of honour or the judges sit. Some sources have also used the term kamiza or joseki.

There are two KATA AXES. The longitudinal kata axis runs through the kata area and is the line along which the kata is performed. The lateral axis is the line down the middle of the kata area directly away from the shomen. For the sake of simplicity, the term kata axis is used in this book, when the direction is obvious.

Sometimes a central area is also defined, which is about two metres in diameter in the centre of the kata.

8 x 8 m kata area

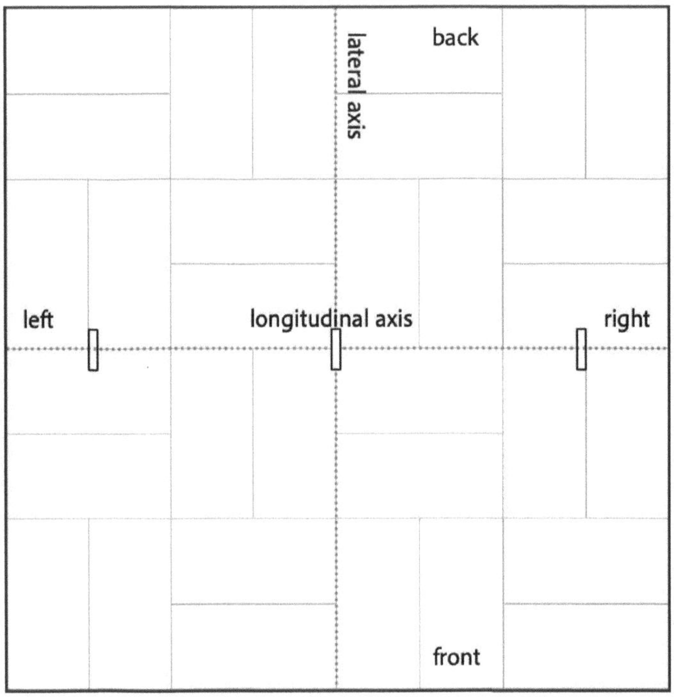

SHOMEN

The BOWING POSITIONS are on the longitudinal kata axis. The kata is started with a bow at the edge of the kata area. The bowing positions in the kata area are often marked by tapes with a distance of six metres between the outer edges of the tapes. The centre of the kata area is also marked with a tape. Before performing and after closing the kata there is also a bowing when entering and leaving the tatami.

What may be confusing is that in the Kodokan kata textbooks all distances are given in the old Japanese measurements. In Japan the size of a tatami is about 0.9×1.8 m instead of 1×2 m as in other parts of the world. As a result, the kata area is also smaller in Kodokan textbooks. For example, the starting distance is 5.4 metres instead of six metres as is the case internationally.

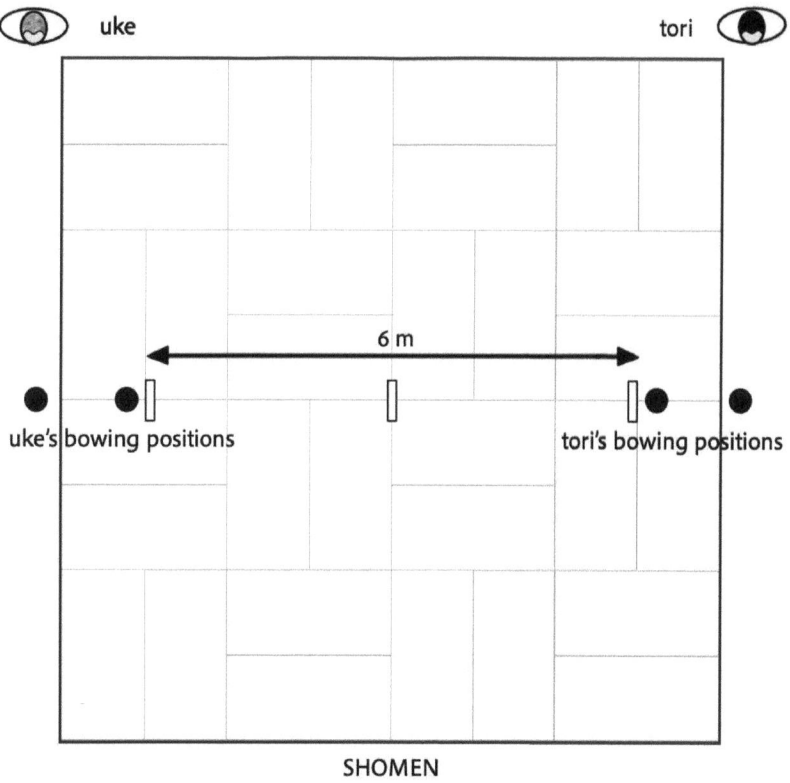

SHOMEN

COMMON FEATURES OF RANDORI-NO-KATA

THINGS TO BE NOTED IN PERFORMANCE

A good kata involves both parties being fully present mentally. The mental attitude must guide all physical activity. Both tori and uke must exude inner calm, alertness and self-confidence. Kata should not be done only as a technical performance. Both must have good posture, and the bodies must not be stiff.

In kata, the judogi should be clean, intact and white. Blue judogi is reserved for shiai, where colour distinguishes the fighters. In the belt, it is advisable to use the so-called kata knot (1, 2), which is stronger than a normal knot. In competitions, the belt must not cross at the back (3) and its ends should be 20 to 30 cm long and of equal length (2). Ensure trouser strings are not visible by tucking them inside the trousers.

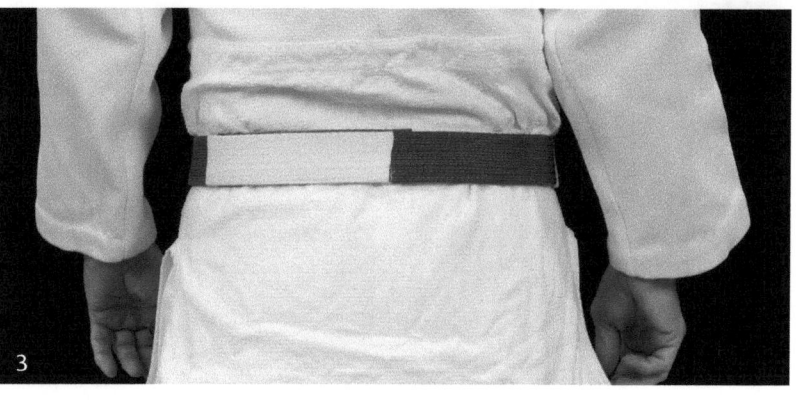

Nage-no-kata and katame-no-kata are performed silently and in an expressionless manner. Signalling with different sounds or gestures is not appropriate. However, an exception can be allowed for those judokas for whom signalling is necessary. In this case, for example, clapping or other agreed signals are used. The audience following the kata should also be silent. Any possible applause is only given after the closing ceremonies and not at all during the grading examinations.

The movement forward to the starting position of the techniques takes place always with the left foot. The movement backwards is started with the right foot.

The kata must be harmonious in rhythm and speed. This is achieved by the fact that movements and executions take place at the same tempo throughout the kata. In addition, small pauses calm the kata. However, there are rhythm changes within the individual techniques.

The movement becomes more rhythmic when you exhale just before starting to move. It relaxes the upper body and shoulders.

You can only learn a good kata by practising and performing the kata as much as possible. By participating in demonstrations and competitions, you can get confidence in your performance.

OPENING AND CLOSING CEREMONIES The opening and closing ceremonies of nage-no-kata and katame-no-kata are the same for bows. Tori sets the rhythm and uke follows so that the movements are almost simultaneous.

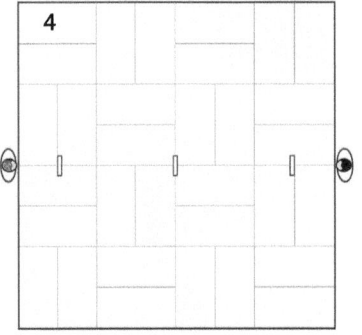

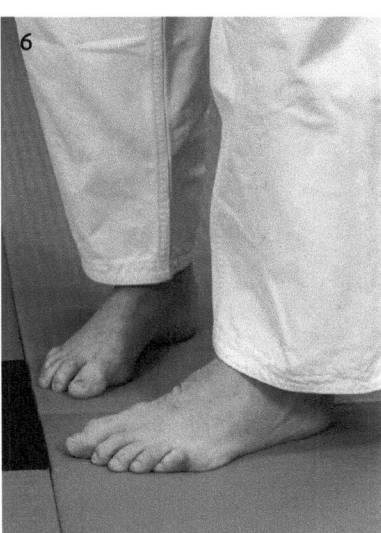
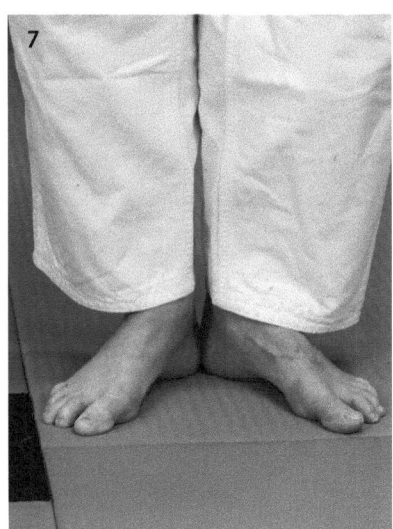

BEGINNING OF KATA

Tori and uke enter the tatami at a point from which they can walk directly to the starting position. Tori stands on the right and uke on the left, both waiting at the corners of the kata area, heels together and facing the shomen. (p. 31). After receiving permission, they walk to their starting positions on the sides of the kata area and turn to face each other (4). Walking is normal way of walking.

Tori and uke bow towards the centre of the kata area (8). The kata presentation begins with this standing bow and ends when leaving the area with a standing bow at the same point.

After the bowing, tori and uke continue to walk towards each other to a distance of six metres apart from each other and stop. The heels are together and the hands gently pressed to the sides (5). Six metres line must not yet be crossed.

Both simultaneously turn to face the shomen. Tori turns counter-clockwise and uke clockwise. The turn is made in two steps at the same time so that after the turn tori's and uke's toes are in the same line (6, 7). Then the pair makes a standing bow (9).

Then tori and uke turn towards each other. Both have their heels together and the kata axis is between the feet. Both go simultaneously down to the kneeling position and perform a kneeling bow (10). After the bowing, tori and uke stand up. The heels are still together.

STANDING AND KNEELING BOW

At the start of the STANDING BOW, the posture is good and the hands and fingers are straight and together at the sides. Fingertips are lightly pressing the trousers (11). When bowing the hands are slid along the thighs to the front of the legs until the fingertips touch just above the knee. The upper body bends from the pelvis about 30 degrees. The back is straight and the head is in line with the back. The gaze is aligned approximately 2 m along the tatami (12, 13). The Bow is made slower down than up (e.g. down one-two-three and up one-two). When straightening up, the hands slide back to the sides of the thighs. It is important that tori and uke bow with the same rhythm and that the rhythm of all bows remains the same. The total duration of the bow is about four seconds.

The BOW IN THE KNEELING POSITION is performed by first kneeling on the left knee. The knee comes in the same place as the left foot was before. Then the right knee is also brought down onto the tatami (14). The ball of the foot is against the mat. Next, the insteps are straightened to be in contact with the mat (15) and the judoka sits with the back straight down on the heels (16). The distance between the knees is about two fist widths. The feet are in a position where the big toes are slightly overlapping.

In bowing, the hands are slid along the thighs to the tatami about two fist widths apart from the knees. The fingers are outstretched and together. The distance between the fingertips is about one fist width apart. The bowing is made with the back

straight and the forehead is kept about 30-40 cm from the hands.

The gaze is directed about one metre into the tatami. The head is not bent down during the bowing, but the neck remains almost straight. The line between head and back is straight and horizontal. The buttocks remain close to the heels (17). The speed of the bow is the same as in a standing bow and the descent is slower than when going up.

Standing up is done in reverse order. First, the back is straightened upwards (18) and the insteps are against the tatami, and the balls of the feet are moved to be against the mat (19). Next the **ri**ght

knee is raised up (20) and the judoka stands up on the right foot to a standing position. After standing up, the heels are together.

OPENING AND CLOSING STEP

After bowing, both simultaneously step forward and stop in the shizen-hontai (22-25). In the opening step, the left foot slides along the surface of the mat (24). Right foot is brought behind in the same way without lifting it off the mat. When starting the step, lean slightly forward (23), so that the centre of gravity moves forward and the step becomes natural and not a leap. After the step the hands are relaxed at the sides and no longer pressed into the trousers (25). If the starting positions are marked with tapes,

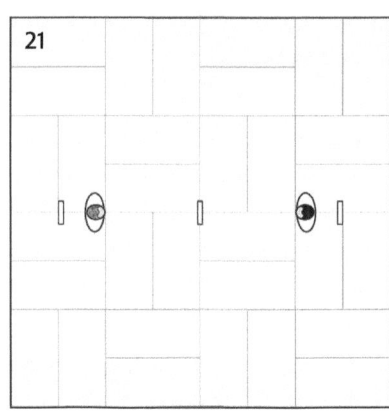

the opening step starts from behind the marker. The opening step should not exceed the width of one mat. After the opening step tori and uke stand in shizen-hontai at a distance of about four metres from each other (21).

END OF THE KATA

At the end of nage-no-kata and katame-no-kata, tori and uke stand in shizentai about four metres from each other (21). Then both take a backward step (25-27) starting with the right foot. The step is of the same length as the opening step forward. After this step, posture is good, heels are together and fingers are again pressing lightly on the trousers. The closing step should end behind the six-metre line. Here too, you should lean backwards and take the step naturally.

After the closing step, tori and uke go down and make a kneeling bow (28). When they have finished, they stand up simultaneously, turn towards the shomen, make a simultaneous standing bow (29) and turn back towards each other. Then they both step backwards, right foot first and move backwards over to the edge of the kata area and make a standing bow in the direction of the kata area (30). This concludes the kata and in grading examination or competition the evaluation of the kata.

In competitions, return to the edge of the mat is done the same route as it was entered. After the bows tori and uke may turn their backs to the shomen and leave the tatami walking normally. Although the kata has ended, any behaviour contrary to the spirit of judo before leaving the mat can still lead to disqualification in grading examination or in competition.

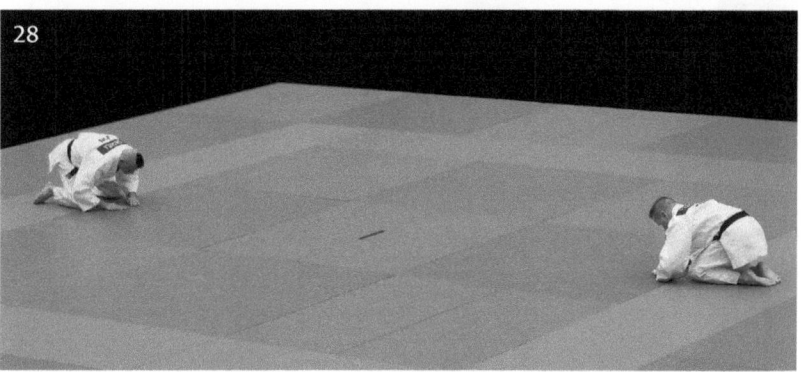

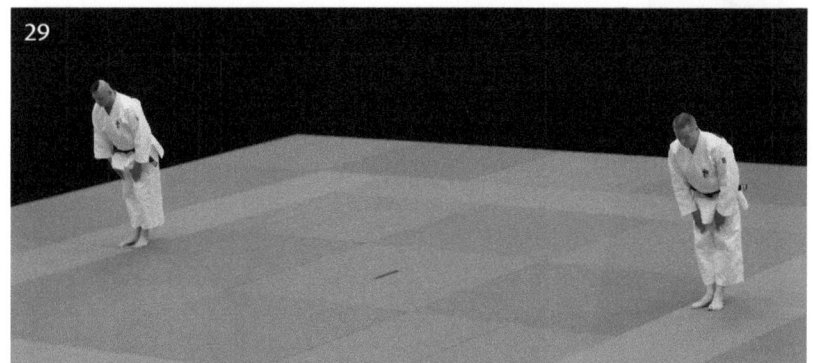

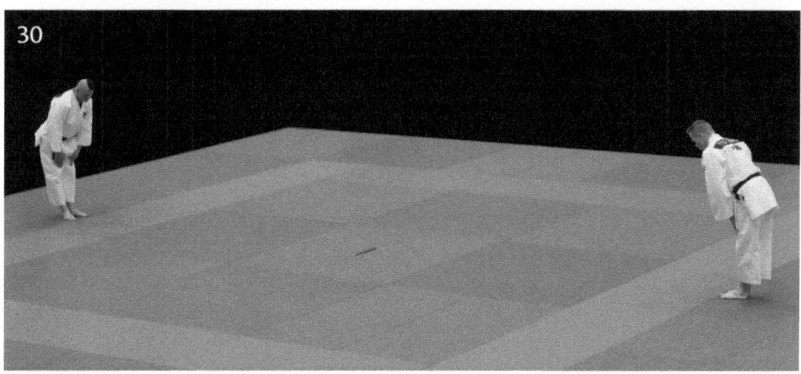

投の形

NAGE-NO-KATA

GENERAL

The original versions of nage-no-kata and katame-no-kata had each ten techniques. More detailed notes of the content of the first ten years of the kata have not survived. Due to a long history, each kata contains one currently banned technique in competitions.

From the earliest remaining sources it can be seen that the nage-no-kata has included five waza (groups of techniques): te-waza (hand throwing), koshi-waza (hip throws), ashi-waza (leg throws), ma-sute-mi-waza (sacrifice throws on the back) and yoko-sutemi-waza (sacrifice throws on the side).

The list published in 1895 included the following throws:

Te-waza: uki-otoshi, seoi-nage, SUMI-OTOSHI
Koshi-waza: uki-goshi, harai-goshi, tsurikomi-goshi
Ashi-waza: okuri-ashi-harai, sasae-tsurikomi-ashi, uchi-mata
Ma-sutemi-waza: tomoe-nage, ura-nage, TSURI-OTOSHI
Yoko-sutemi-waza: yoko-gake or yoko-guruma, uki-waza, TANI-OTOSHI

There is no exact description of tsuri-otoshi. Historical records of the throw are contradictory. Sumi-otoshi was replaced for a while by sukui-nage, which was soon replaced by the more spectacular and physically more

Uki-goshi.

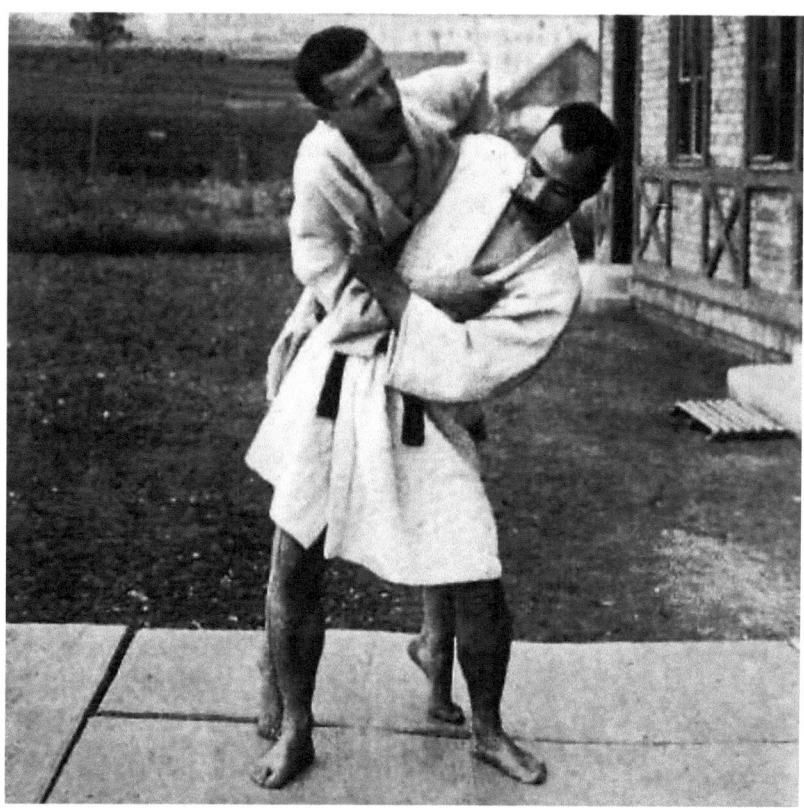

demanding kata-guruma. At the same time, tani-otoshi was dropped off from yoko-sutemi-waza. After the changes, nage-no-kata did not have any backwards going throws. When tsuri-otoshi was replaced to sumi-gaeshi, nage-no-kata had taken its present form in 1906.

Earlier strikes were made with only one step. Most often the second strike was made from the same place where uke was after the ukemi. Kano changed the strikes to two steps to give them more power. After the 1930s, the starting positions of the strikes became established as they are today.

NAGE-NO-KATA TECHNIQUES

Each waza is demonstrated with three selected throws, shown both as right (migi) and left (hidari) techniques. All kata embody the principles of judo—the best and most efficient use of energy. This is why kuzushi movements in nage-no-kata are very subtle. However, they are sufficient to achieve a technically clean throw.

The techniques of nage-no-kata are:

TE-WAZA
1. Uki-otoshi
2. Seoi-nage
3. Kata-guruma

KOSHI-WAZA
1. Uki-goshi
2. Harai-goshi
3. Tsurikomi-goshi

ASHI-WAZA
1. Okuri-ashi-harai
2. Sasae-tsurikomi-ashi
3. Uchi-mata

MA-SUTEMI-WAZA
1. Tomoe-nage
2. Ura-nage
3. Sumi-gaeshi

YOKO-SUTEMI-WAZA
1. Yoko-gake
2. Yoko-guruma
3. Uki-waza

A shortened version of the nage-no-kata can also be performed in which either one or three groups of techniques are presented, starting closing formalities after the last left-side throw. In this book, only the first throw of each technique is explained. The second throw is performed as a mirror image of the first and changing the sides. Uki-goshi is the only throw that is performed first as a left-handed throw.

NAGE-NO-KATA STUDYING ACCORDING TO THE IJF

The IJF has published a teaching package for the first three wazas of the nage-no-kata. The aim is to provide the concept and tools to bring kata closer to everyday judo practice. For each technique the starting points are based on principles. The teaching does not follow the order of the kata, but to learn the easiest throws first.

The concept teaches the general technical basis of the kata. Only after judoka understands the technical basis correctly, the drill can be moved on to the practice of the entire kata according to the strict form it requires.

The model given has three stages. Before the first stage the judoka must already know the basics, such as the bows, postures, grips, ukemi and movements. In each stage, the judoka chooses three throws to practice.

The exercises for the first nine techniques in this book are based on the IJF model.

PERFORMING NAGE-NO-KATA

Both tori and uke will ensure that the kata techniques are performed approximately in the middle of the kata area without interruption.

Tori determines the starting points of the techniques by going to the right position and waiting for uke to arrive at the correct attacking

FLOW CHART

AGE and LEVEL	Pre-Stage Before 11 Years Old or Green Belt	11-12 Years old and/or Green Belt	13-14 Years old and/or Blue Belt	15-16 Years old and/or Brown Belt	
	Requirements	3 techniques Static or from movement	6 techniques From movement or in Kata-style	9 techniques Idealy in Kata style	Black Belt
	Phase 0	Phase 1	Phase 2	Phase 3	

NAGE-NO KATA 3 FIRST GROUPS TE-WAZA, KOSHI-WAZA AND ASHI-WAZA

FROM THE TECHNIQUE TO THE KATA

SOURCE:IJF NAGE-NO-KATA EDUCATIVE PROJECT 2022. HOW TO TEACH NAGE-NO-KATA TO BEGINNERS

The dark grey ones are the techniques recommended for the stage and light grey ones are possible under certain conditions.

RECOMMENDED TECHNIQUES FOR THE DIFFERENT STAGES			
TECHNIQUE	STAGE 1	STAGE 2	STAGE 3
Uki-otoshi	X		
Seoi-nage	X		
Kata-guruma		(X)	X
Uki-goshi	X	X	
Harai-goshi		X	
Tsurikomi-goshi			X
Okuri-ashi-harai		(X)	X
Sasae-tsurikomi-ashi	X	X	
Uchi-mata		(X)	X

distance. Uke initiates the action by taking a grip or going for a strike. Tori reacts to the attack at the last moment. Tori's reaction often happens so fast that it seems almost simultaneous to uke's attack.

All throws should show the different stages of the throw (kuzushi, tsukuri and kake). They are not necessarily sequential but may be overlapping or simultaneous.

In the throw, tori supports uke and guides uke to a safe ukemi position. If necessary, he brings the other hand to help but does not take a grip with it. The knees are slightly flexible (1). After the throw, tori is in a good stable position and controls uke. Tori holds the position for a moment with the face towards uke (zanshin) and then moves on to the next throw.

The movements of tori and uke before the engagement are described for each technique. The second throw is a mirror image of the first. If the first technique is started with the left foot, the second one is started with the right foot.

The role of uke is important. Uke who is too active or otherwise helps tori all the time can ruin the whole performance. The same effect is if uke is too stiff or loose.

During the transitions in the kata, the back is usually not turned towards the shomen. An exception is made by uke when he stands up from ukemi. Uke should also avoid passing between tori and the shomen when moving into position.

There are no guidelines for the duration of the kata. Each couple determines their own rhythm with which the kata is performed. Nage-no-kata typically lasts 6-7:30 minutes.

Uke and tori can calm down the rhythm of the kata by pausing for a short moment before uke's initiative. Often a small exhalation is sufficient before starting the movement. The only exception is the first throw of ura-nage, which uke starts as soon as he gets up from the hidari-tomoe-nage.

A good kata can be recognised by the fact that the movements are technically correct, and both show excellent body control. The most typical mistake is that the movement is wavy and stiff when the pair tries to follow a prearranged choreography and exact steps. If the body is loose and insecure, it further undermines the overall impression of competence. It is also a mistake if uke prepares the throw in advance by twisting his body in the direction of the incoming throw. The feet must stay on their own rails.

Typical mistakes of tori are that preparatory actions for the throw are not visible, kuzushi is weak or does not exist, the timing of the throw is wrong and too much force is used. Tori must learn to use the force of full body correctly. Excessive use of the arms or upper body leads to stiff shoulders. At the same time, it makes movements slow. Tori must not anticipate his reaction to uke's attack. Corrective steps are a sign of poor balance.

Uke's mistakes include wrong distances, incomplete or poor attacking, jumping to ukemi and holding a grip on tori's judogi until the end of the throw.

Many of these mistakes are easy to correct. The more difficult ones to correct are those where you have to get the technical execution right first. Often these require active forgetting of the previous way of doing.

IMPORTANT ELEMENTS OF NAGE-NO-KATA

POSITIONS AND DISTANCES

Nage-no-kata techniques are started either from uke's side, with uke stepping a bit closer to the centre or symmetrically from the centre of the kata area. Exceptions to this are the hidari-okuri-ashi-harai and the techniques with a strike while uke is moving: the hidari-uki-goshi and migi-ura-nage. The starting position of the tomoe-nage is defined to be on uke's side approximately one metre from the centre line. More exact positions are given later in the text for each technique. For the second technique the position is a mirror image of the previous position. During the kata, the positions do not change very much.

The grip distance between pairs is about 60 cm and depends on the size of the pair. The initial distance should be such that uke must take a half step forward when reaching to get a grip on tori's lapel. For the okuri-ashi-harai the distance is about 30 cm. The striking distance is defined as 1,8 m, but for most larger judokas, two metres is an appropriate distance. The starting distance for techniques performed in the jigotai is about 90 cm.

STANCES AND GRIPS

SHIZEN-HONTAI is the natural basic stance (2). It should be upright, with the hands relaxed at the sides. The feet are shoulder-width apart, and the weight is evenly distributed on both feet. Shizen-hontai is taken after the opening step and before the start of each technique.

MIGI/HIDARI-SHIZENTAI (basic posture right or left foot in front) the basic grip of the judogi is taken. One hand is on the sleeve and the other on the lapel (3). Exceptions are tsurikomi-goshi and jigotai stances. The grip on the judogi must be firm and at the same time light, without a tight compression with fingers. The hands are relaxed and slightly hooked.

The JIGOTAI (defensive posture) is used in two techniques: sumi-gaeshi and uki-waza. In jigotai the right hand is taken under the partner's left armpit to his back. Fingers are pointing slightly upwards. The left hand is holding palm open partner's upper arm from below. No grip is taken on the sleeve. The knees are bent and heads are side by side. Heads do not touch each other. The upper bodies are slightly tilted forward. The back is straight (4). The stance of tori and uke is similar.

Jigotai is not a purely defensive posture. Although the legs are spread and the hips are lowered, the posture must allow free movement of the legs and unrestricted rotation of the body. Both are needed to unbalance the opponent's position. In jigotai tori and uke hold each other lightly, and weight is slightly behind. Before moving, there is a slight tension but no pull between tori and uke.

MOVEMENT

In nage-no-kata there are two ways of moving: ayumi-ashi and tsugi-ashi. In both movements, the soles of the feet are all the time in light contact with the tatami and the weight is more on the ball of the foot than the heels. The feet are not brought together laterally (6, 8).

Ayumi-ashi (5, 6) is an alternating stepping walk, where the feet slide along the surface of the tatami and pass each other. The hands are relaxed without swinging at the sides, and posture is good. Ayumi-ashi is used after the opening step as an approach step before the techniques. The exception is the transition from hidari-tomoe-nage to migi-ura-nage.

In tsugi-ashi (7, 8), the feet move along their own paths from shizentai to shizentai. The feet do not pass each other and remain at least half a foot's length apart (7). In tsugi-ashi, the weight is lowered slightly lower than in ayumi-ashi and the knees are kept flexible. Tsugi-ashi is used when there is a grip and tori and uke move together. An exception to this is the beginning of tomoe-nage and movements in jigotai posture. In movement the centre of gravity must be moved, not just the feet. The hands remain relaxed and slightly hooked during the movement.

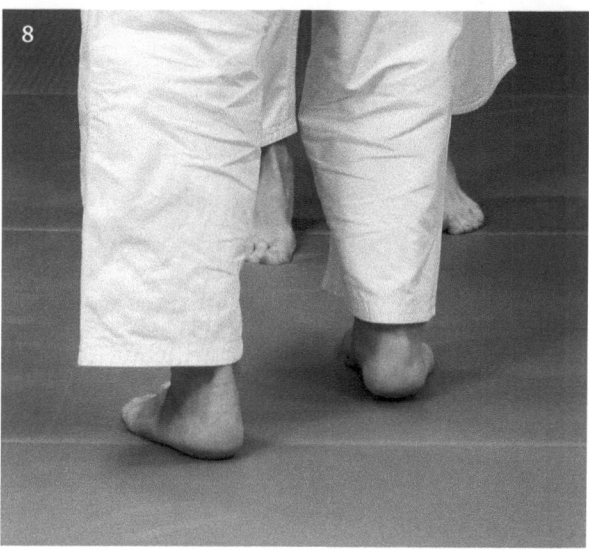

FOCUSING THE GAZE

During executions and transitions, both have a neutral facial expression and a focused, straight ahead gaze (2). Gaze is directed somewhere in the distance. During transitions, you need to perceive where you are going. Neither looks around nor turns his head looking for the right spot.

THE ROLE OF UKE

Uke must react to tori's unbalancing acts naturally and often only as to regain a balance. Eventually he ends up in a throwing situation, where tori can make the throw cleanly and efficiently. After taking a grip or in a striking attack uke must at all times keep his body tense, seeking to maintain his balance and be passive in terms of tori's throwing actions. An exception to this is yoko-guruma, where uke counters the ura-nage.

UKEMI

At the end of the throw, uke releases his grip on tori's judogi. Uke must land from the ukemi with body and legs straight (9). On the mat the beating is performed normally and the arm remains straight on the mat or close to the mat. In techniques where uke rises from ukemi to a standing position uke must stop directly in place, without any corrective steps.

9

Standing up from an ukemi from the mat

Uke should come up from ukemi in the direction of the beating hand and move from there directly to the starting position of the next technique. When standing up and during the transition uke's back may be momentarily towards the shomen. It is recommended that standing up is done by bending the knee on the side of the beating hand by placing the foot under the other leg, placing the hands on the knees (10) and coming first to the kneeling position (11) and then to standing. Do not use hands to push up from the tatami.

UKE'S STRIKING ATTACK

In four techniques, uke attacks by striking tori on the head (tento). These techniques are seoi-nage, uki-goshi, ura-nage and yoko-guruma.

In all cases the strike is similar and is made with two steps. Uke must seek a distance so that he can reach to strike tori in a balanced position on the head. In uki-goshi and ura-nage, uke starts the strike directly from the walk. In all four techniques, uke attacks first with the right hand strike.

Before the strike, uke clenches both of his hands into a fist. The thumb is on the fingers (13). Uke steps forward with his left foot and raises his right hand, his arm slightly bent next to the ear and straight up. He does not twist his body backwards. Then uke steps forward with his right foot and tries to hit tori on the top of his head (12). The strike is directed from the top down and is made with the side of the fist (13). Throughout the strike uke must be in good balance and his weight not too much on the foot in front.

Uke's body does not twist or bend forward. Uke's gaze is directed straight ahead throughout the strike and towards tori. The strike doesn't need to be particularly fast, but it must be realistic enough. Uke balances the blow by bringing his free hand slightly forward in a natural position.

The strike can be practised first with one step and then with two. To start with, tori can hold his hands together with the palms facing outwards on the top of his head and uke strikes tori's hands (15). First practice with a slow strike, and as the training progresses, the pace is increased. It is particularly important practising the correct distance and rhythm. The distance is correct when uke does not have to reach for the blow.

The power of the strike must be directed at the point of impact and the path must be such that the strike stops almost as soon as it reaches its target. The strike does not continue downwards and uke does not lose his balance even if tori directs the strike to the side.

13

14

15

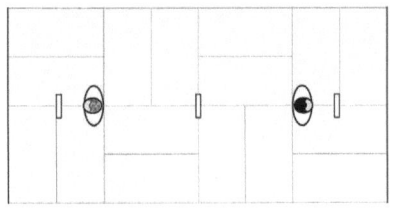

ADJUSTING THE JUDOGI

Tori and uke will ensure that the judogi is neatly worn throughout the whole kata. The judogi can be discreetly adjusted and the belt can be tightened from one technique to the next. However, the judogi must not be constantly fixed. The actual adjusting is done after each technique group, when tori and uke stand four metres apart with their backs to each other.

The most elegant way to do the adjustment is to first take hold of the front of the jacket and pulling downwards in one pull (16) and then the back of the jacket with a single pull (17) and finally straighten and tighten the belt. The belt must not be detached and tied again during the kata. This is a big mistake in competitions.

After the judogi has been adjusted tori turns clockwise and uke turns counter-clockwise. At this point, neither may turn his back to the shomen. Turning after the judogi adjustment is done in three steps (19, 20). Turning towards each other should be done simultaneously.

16

Te-waza

The official naming of judo throws is done by the technical department of Kodokan. Some names indicate their nature, like ashi-guruma referring to tori's leg and hiza-guruma to uke's knee. Throws are categorized by tori's actions, such as hand throws or hip throws, though no throw relies solely on one aspect. The group of hip throws is easy to identify, because the names of all the throws allowed in the competition are followed by a goshi. In order to classify the other throws, you need to know their principle and the correct performance. Many throws can fall into two categories especially if the action is slightly altered.

Te-waza includes hand throws UKI-OTOSHI (1), SEOI-NAGE (2) and KATA-GURUMA (3).

2. Seoi-nage

1. Uki-otoshi

3. Kata-guruma

UKI-OTOSHI

Uki-otoshi has remained unchanged in the nage-no-kata since the days of Jigoro Kano. As a throw, it is rarely seen in randori or shiai, but the principles it sets out can be applied to other techniques. Uki-otoshi is a demanding technique, especially for uke. Uke must be able and have the courage to make a forward ukemi.

PRINCIPLE

Tori increases the distance from uke and uke gets off balance. Tori's last long step and the descent down contain a surprise that increases the distance more. Uke does not notice this and starts to step forward a normal step. Simultaneously tori pulls down. Uke does not have time to change the length of his step and is thrown.

TEACHING

Uki-otoshi teaches tori how to react to uke's movement coming towards him, to make kuzushi by changing the length of the steps, to throw just at the right moment, and to use the full strength of the body to throw and not to throw by using only the pull of the hands. For uke, it teaches the forward ukemi without a support point in front of uke. The same situation is repeated, for example, in sasae-tsurikomi-ashi.

KUZUSHI

Kuzushi is done with the body by increasing the distance.

IMPORTANT

Tori needs to pull down as uke's foot is just touching the tatami.

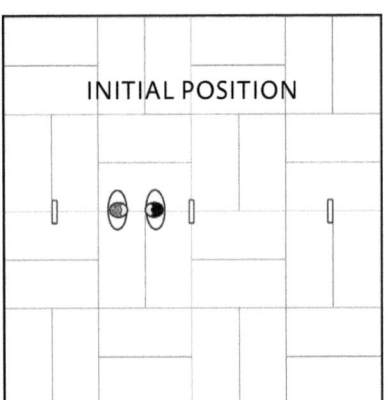

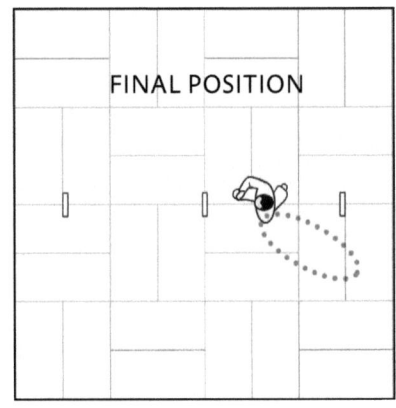

EXECUTION

After the kneeling bow, tori and uke stand up simultaneously (1). Starting with his left foot (2) tori walks to uke using ayumi-ashi.

Before tori has reached the engagement distance, uke starting with his left foot (3) takes a couple of short ayumi-ashi steps, so that they stop at the same time at a distance of about 60 cm apart (4, 5). The place is about one metre from the lateral kata-axis.

The first step is the same in all of the attacks where tori moves backwards with three tsugi-ashi steps. Uke's intention is to take a grip of tori in migi-shiz-entai. Uke starts to step with his right foot a step of about half a step and takes the grip. Tori reacts to the situation, takes a step back with his left foot and takes grip of uke's judogi during his step (6). Tori moves off backwards before uke has time to get a good grip of tori. In order to get a good grip, uke has to stretch his step and reach out a little forward (7). Tori now pulls his right foot back, ending the first tsugi-ashi step. Uke wants to keep his balance and follows with a left foot tsugi-ashi step. After the step he is, however, slightly off balance forward and has a weaker balance than tori (6-8). Tori has taken the initiative.

Tori's own movement is an enticement for uke to follow. If he would start pulling hard with his hands uke's first reaction would be to resist the pull.

Tori starts again with his left foot a tsugi-ashi backwards. This step is a few centimetres longer than the first (9). Uke wants to respond and takes a tsugi-ashi forward to maintain his balance. However, uke does not notice tori's longer step and becomes a little bit more forward off balance (10).

Tori starts for the third time with his left foot a step backwards (11). While uke responds to tori's movement and is about to step with his right foot the third step forward of the same length, tori surprises uke. He stretches his left leg step far back, bringing the ball of his foot to the tatami, brings uke off balance and puts his left knee on the tatami (15). The knee comes to the mat slightly on the shomen side of the kata axis and the toes are on the right side of the axis. The shin is approximately 30 to 45 degrees angle to the kata axis. Tori's stance is stable when the supporting points of the feet form a triangle (12).

Tori throws uke by pulling with both hands strongly diagonally downwards (12-18). Both hands pull in the same direction. Right hand pulls towards the left hip and the left hand in the same line in the direction of the throw. The pull is made with tori's descending movement and with the hands (13, 14). There is no rotational movement of the hands.

Tori has to increase the distance and start pulling downwards at the exact same moment as uke's advancing foot is touching the tatami. Most important is that the pull takes place at a moment when uke does not have opportunity to lengthen his step anymore. The pull must not be left so late that uke already has his weight completely on the foot.

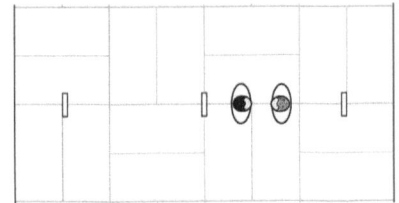

After the throw, tori stands up and moves to a position about one metre from the centre line on the right-hand side of it. His back is towards the centre and he remains waiting for uke. The place is a mirror image of the previous throw. Uke stands up and walks to the front of tori at a suitable distance. Then uke tries to grip tori in hidari-shizentai and they start to left the left-hand uki-otoshi in the same way as before.

!

It is important that tori's second step creates a little more distance to uke. This way uke is already slightly off balance before the last step. The throw becomes easier, and tori doesn't have to leave all the work to the last step

Special attention should be paid to the timing of the throw and the length of uke's last step. If uke takes a longer step, or if he is given the opportunity to lengthen his step then kuzushi is weak and the throw will not be natural.

* For training purposes uki-otoshi can be practised step by step, with all exercises done on both sides.

Tori and uke face each other with palms touching and lean against each other with straight bodies (19). Tori turns to the side, and uke performs a forward ukemi on the mat (20). Next, from the same starting position, tori steps back with his left foot and descends on his left knee. Uke makes a ukemi on the mat (21).

In the second phase, tori and uke are in shizentai and take grip on each other. Tori brings his left knee to the mat and pulls uke downwards. Uke makes a soft ukemi while circling around to the side. Then the same thing is done while moving backwards. Finally, uki-otoshi is done with a hard ukemi.

Kata techniques can also be practiced from a sideways or free movement, focusing on finding the right moment to create distance and throw uke. There's no need to bring the knee to the mat—it's all about kuzushi and timing. Similarly, it is worth exploring how to apply the same principle to sumi-otoshi.

SEOI-NAGE Seoi-nage has remained almost the same in the kata since the beginning. It is done from uke's striking attack. Even though the throw is previously familiar to those learning kata, what's new is uke's strike and the time pressure it puts on tori to make the entry of the throw quickly.

PRINCIPLE
Tori utilizes the movement of the attacking uke using the shoulder as a support point and throws uke by levering him straight over. Nage-no-kata presents a pure hand throw and its principle. As a randori technique, in seoi-nage the hands and hips work together and a twist of the body is also performed.

TEACHING
Seoi-nage teaches the right timing for tori to meet uke's attack. It also teaches how to use uke's forward movement to perform kuzushi and a full-speed tai-sabaki forward.

KUZUSHI
Kuzushi is performed by pulling uke's striking arm forward.

IMPORTANT
Tori must make a timely tsukuri in.

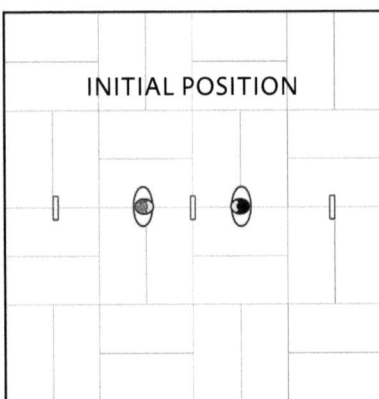

INITIAL POSITION

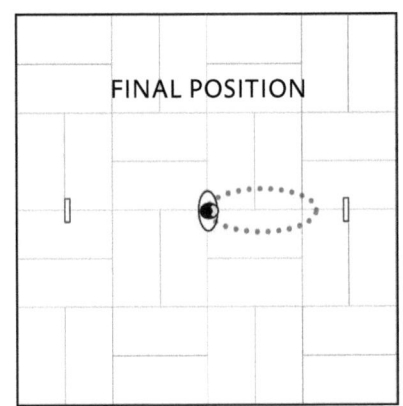

FINAL POSITION

EXECUTION

Tori and uke face each other in the centre of the kata area a little less than two metres apart (1).

Uke starts the attack forward. He takes a step with his left foot, while at the same time lifting his right fist above his head (2), takes a step with his right foot and tries to strike from above at the top of tori's head (3).

Tori moves his right foot to the inside and in front of uke's right foot, places the palm of his left hand on uke's upper arm, guides uke's right arm with his hand slightly up and forward and takes a grip on uke's elbow bend or slightly above (4). Tori starts to counter the strike at the moment the strike has started and there is no time for uke to change his attack.

Tori pulls with his left hand to the front to break uke's balance forward. As a result of the kuzushi uke is forced to take a step to correct his balance with his left foot. Uke also tries to block the throw by bringing the palm of his left hand and placing it on tori's left hip (6).

Tori pivots on the ball of his right foot to the left bringing his left foot to the inside of uke's left foot, bends his knees and turns his back to uke (5, 6). At the same time, tori brings his right hand under uke's armpit onto his shoulder and takes hold of it. If tori's kuzushi is successful, uke's feet are now parallel (7).

Tori pulls uke's chest and stomach firmly against his back. Uke's heels are now slightly off the tatami and uke is leaning forward (8).

8

Tori bends his upper body forward, straightens both knees and throws uke by pulling downwards with both hands (9-11). The throw is made by levering straight over the shoulder without the upper body rotation. At the end of the throw, tori does not bend knees but bends his upper body forward and supports uke with almost straight legs (12, 13).

After the throw, tori moves to the starting position of the hidari throw about one metre left from the centre line and waits for uke. Uke stands up, moves to within striking distance of tori, waits a moment, then starts attacking with his left hand strike in the same way as before. Tori does a left seoi-nage.

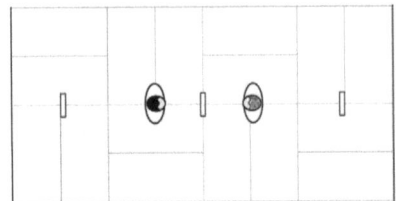

! Tori may not counter uke's strike by stopping the hand. Tori uses his hand to prevent the strike hitting the head. At the same time, tori grabs the inside of uke's arm above the elbow and makes kuzushi. Kuzushi and tai-sabaki are almost simultaneous. Kuzushi starts a little earlier and continues for the duration of tai-sabaki. In seoi-nage it is particularly difficult to get the timing to work so that kuzushi is real and uke is forced to take a step with his left foot. Uke must not take this step independently, but tori has to force uke to take the step.

Uke must maintain his balance during the strike. If he loses his balance to the front then all tori has to do is to turn and go under uke and throw.

Tori's right hand must come on uke's shoulder. Sometimes seoi-nage was taught in a way in which uke lost his balance in the strike and the throw was also made as a clear ippon-seoi-nage with the right hand on biceps and with a strong twist. Nowadays there is a return to the more original form and its principle.

Some books suggest that uke is learning during the kata and therefore in the next technique the strike would always be slightly different. However, this does not correspond to current teaching.

13

✱ Seoi-nage can be practised step by step, increasing the speed gradually. At the beginning uke stands with his arms stretched out (14). Tori steps with his right foot, bringing his left hand to the crook of uke's elbow, does tai-sabaki and takes a light grip (15).

Next, uke begins to fall forward with arms outstretched (16). Tori does tai-sabaki in, takes a light grip and lifts uke slightly in the air (17). The idea is to get the timing right when uke falls forward. Uke should be well balanced on the back of tori. It is particularly important that tori does not collide with uke. As an intermediate step tori can practice to bring the right hand to uke's shoulder and lift (18, 19).

The next step is to make a one-step strike. Uke stands with left foot in front and arm up. Uke takes a step with his right foot forward and makes a slow strike. The strike must hit the head.

Tori comes in for the throw, makes kuzushi and lifts uke into the air. When tori makes kuzushi, he forces uke to take a step with his left foot forward. At the same time, uke places the palm of his left hand on tori's hips. Finally you can try to throw.

The last step is to practise the whole performance. Uke makes a strike with two steps. Tori enters in for the throw, does kuzushi and finally throws uke. Slowly at first, then with a bit of higher speed. As the speed increases, neither should lose focus on the precision of the technique.

Instead of a strike tori can practice a similar movement in a situation where uke is pushing his hand into tori's neck.

KATA-GURUMA   Kata-guruma is currently not allowed in competitions in its kata form. Different variations of kata-guruma are still used. This throw requires good technical skills and balance control. Although the throw is done technically correct, tori still needs strong legs and midbody for the lift. A beginner can also be intimidated by the high falling ukemi.

PRINCIPLE
Tori creates an opportunity to get below uke's centre of gravity by increasing the distance, pulling the sleeve and using his own positioning to lift uke into the air.

TEACHING
Kata-guruma teaches tori body control, use of the hips and legs and coordination for lifting uke. It also teaches the use of the sleeve hand to make space and to make kuzushi using the movement of uke. For uke it teaches hard ukemi.

KUZUSHI
Kuzushi is done by increasing distance and pulling with the sleeve hand.

IMPORTANT
The tsukuri should be done so that uke's centre of gravity is just above tori.

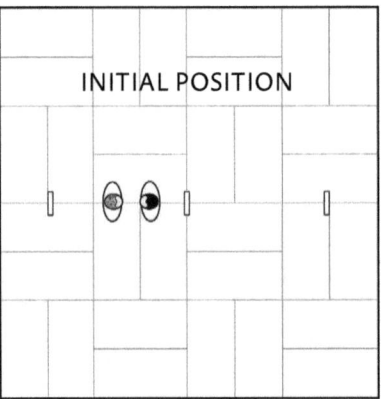

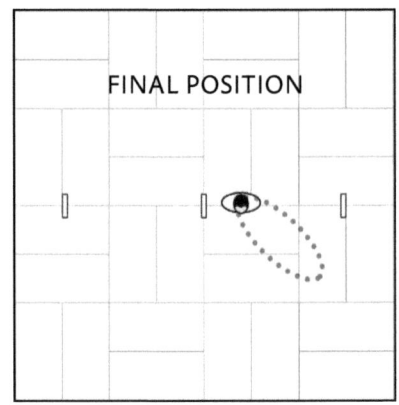

EXECUTION

After the hidari seoi-nage, tori goes to the same starting position as in the uki-otoshi and waits for uke. Tori stands in shizen-hontai and looks straight ahead. Uke gets up from ukemi and comes to about 60 cm from tori (1).

In the same way as in uki-otoshi uke tries to grip tori in migi-shizentai. Tori reacts and moves backwards before uke has got a grip. Both take a tsugi-ashi step and tori takes the initiative (2).

Tori takes another tsugi-ashi backwards. This step is the same length as the first step. During the step he releases the grip of his left hand, rotates the palm of his hand with a wrist movement round to the inside of uke's upper arm and grabs uke's sleeve at the biceps (3, 4). Uke doesn't want to lose his balance and takes a tsugi-ashi step forward as he did with the first step. Due to Tori's change of grip the distance between the pair is now slightly smaller and uke is more off balance forward. Swapping the grip to the inside of uke's hand makes it easier for tori to release uke's lapel hand more easily and make a better kuzushi. At the same time it removes the possibility of strangulation during the lifting phase of the throw.

Tori takes a long step with his left foot backwards, turns his side towards uke, pulling simultaneously diagonally upwards with his left hand and forces uke to take the third step with his right foot forward (5). This step is as long as before. The direction of tori's pull is over the head and slightly from the side of the neck.

Uke is now off balance forward. Tori crouches into a jigotai, places his neck down close to uke's belt and puts his right hand on the inside of uke's right thigh and pulls uke with both hands (6). It is important that tori does not push uke backwards with his neck, but pulls uke into neck contact. The hand on uke's

thigh is outstretched with the fingers around the leg. As tori starts to go down, uke should loosen his grip on tori's lapel and move his hand over tori's forearm. The lift will also be easier if uke brings his left foot at the same level with his right foot before lifting. Uke defends himself by stiffening his body. Uke must not bend his body during the kuzushi from the hips, but must keep himself straight.

Tori will continue the pull with his left hand and pulls uke on his shoulders (7). Uke presses his left hand fingers straight on Tori's back (10). Uke must not push his thumb under tori's belt. Uke supports himself with the palm of his hand against tori's back

for the duration of the lift. Then tori starts to lift (8, 9). The lifting is light as tori positions his body so that his neck is under the centre of gravity of uke. His right ear is below uke's belt. At the end of the lift tori pulls his left leg back close to his right leg into a shizentai. When uke is on tori's shoulders, he stretches out his body horizontally with the legs straight and ankles together straight (9).

After the lift tori can continue straight into the throw without stopping in between. A slight stop is not a mistake either. Kata-guruma is a throw, not a drop down. Tori throws uke by pulling with his left hand down towards his own belt and steering with his right hand to the front left (11–14). Tori should not throw uke just by bending his upper body. At the end of the throw, tori does not bend his knees very much. Tori can make the kake phase easier by slightly turning his shoulder line in the direction of the upcoming throw so that uke's legs start moving and the throw becomes smoother. Uke should not hold his grip on tori's sleeve during ukemi. It's tori's duty to support uke.

The throwing direction is about 30–45 degrees in the direction of the movement.

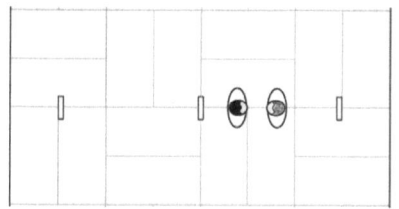

After the throw tori moves to the starting position of the hidari throw to wait for uke. Uke stands up and comes to the front of tori to the right of the shomen. Uke starts to take a grip in hidari-shizentai, and they start kata-guruma on the left side in the same way as before.

! In kata-guruma, tori must come under uke's centre of gravity. This does not happen if tori's left hand does not pull enough to break uke's balance or tori does not squat low enough to the level of uke's belt. He must also not bend forward, but his head, hips and legs must be in the same vertical line. The lift is also difficult if the timing is wrong and the lift is attempted too early. The direction of the throw also shows whether the throw is technically correct or not.

✱ It is a good idea to start the kata-guruma training from a low position. Tori is initially in a transverse kneeling position in front of uke (15). Then tori pulls uke with the sleeve hand on his shoulders and at the same time tori stands up to a higher kneeling position (16). Uke takes support from the back of tori with the palm of his hand. As ukemi becomes quite low uke should turn his head to the left in preparation for ukemi. Tori throws uke from this position (17).

You can also practise uke's balance from a low position. Tori is on all fours crosswise in front of uke. Uke lies on his stomach on tori's back and tries to keep himself straight and with his back arched (18).

The lifting of uke should be taught in stages, starting with one step and using the sleeve hand for assistance (19, 20). Initially, tori will focus only on finding the correct position to go under uke's centre of gravity. From there, you gradually start using both arms and lifting. These exercises are performed as uchi-komi with both hands and on both sides.

Although kata-guruma is currently not allowed in competitions the same principle can be applied to throws, which are performed without gripping below the belt. One option used in competitions is to take a one sided grip and bring the head under uke's armpit. The throw can be made from an upright position or by sacrifice. If sacrificed, the technique is sutemi-waza and technically a variation of uki-waza. The principle of tsukuri and timing is still very similar to kata-guruma in nage-no-kata.

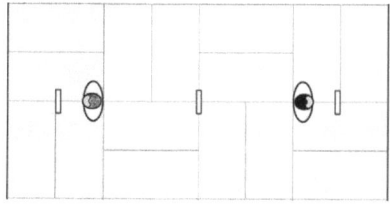

Adjusting the judogi

After the hidari-kata-guruma tori and uke return to their positions after the opening steps. The distance is about four metres from each other and the couple is standing with their backs facing to the centre and they adjust their judogis. Then they turn around, move towards each other and begin the koshi-waza.

If only the first waza of nage-no-kata is performed, then after the adjustment of judogis and the turn, tori and uke start closing ceremonies (see closing formalities) and finish the kata.

KOSHI-WAZA

Jigoro Kano has described how the three koshi-waza throws of the nage-no-kata are interrelated. Shiro Saigo was one of Kano's best students and Kano practiced a lot with him. Kano often succeeded in throwing Saigo with his favourite technique, the UKI-GOSHI (1). Eventually Saigo figured out that by turning to the side he could dodge Kano's throw. Kano thought for a while looking for a suitable solution and finally decided to lift his leg up to block the turn. Thus was born HARAI-GOSHI (2). Saigo took then a while to learn how to counter harai-goshi. His solution was to push his hips forward to prevent a throw over the leg. Now it was Kano's turn to find an answer to this counter, and he decided to drop his weight so low, that even with a little force he could tip Saigo over. Thus was born TSURIKOMI-GOSHI (3). These throws are still in the kata in the same order.

1. Uki-goshi

2. Harai-goshi

3. Tsurikomi-goshi

UKI-GOSHI   Many young judoka have difficulty in perceiving the difference between uki-goshi and o-goshi. In uki-goshi the throw is made with a twist of the body while in o-goshi, and in many other hip throws, the throw is made with the lift of the hip.

Uki-goshi is the only throw in nage-no-kata that is performed first to the left side. It is also the only throw that practices against a right-sided attack with a left-sided technique. The situation corresponds to a match situation where one has the migi-stance and the other has the hidari-stance (kenka-yotsu).

PRINCIPLE
Tori lifts uke with his shoulder, pulls uke to his hip and throws him over the hip by twisting the body. In seoi-nage tori went under the strike and threw a migi-throw. Here is another option to dodge uke's strike to the head by doing a hidari throw.

TEACHING
Uki-goshi teaches tsukuri in a kenka-yotsu situation. At the same time it teaches the use of the hips in a different way from other hip throws.

KUZUSHI
Kuzushi is done by pulling uke towards tori with the hand around uke's waist.

IMPORTANT
Dodging the strike by going under, lifting with the shoulder and use of the hip.

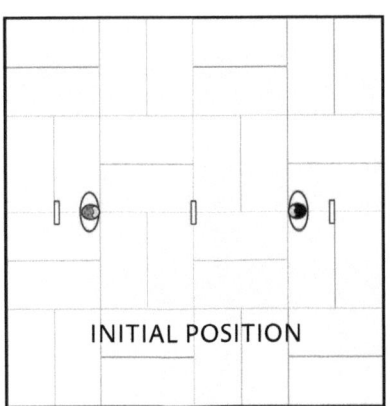

INITIAL POSITION

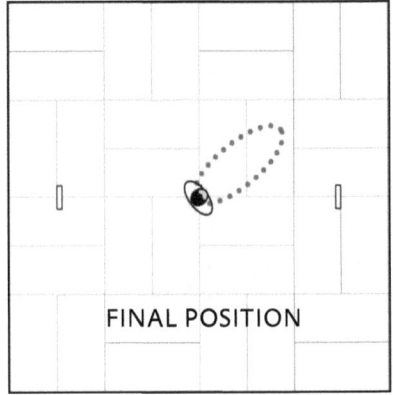

FINAL POSITION

EXECUTION

After adjusting the judogi tori and uke start moving towards each other at the same time (1). When they have come within about two metres of each other, uke starts the attack directly without a stop. Uke takes a step with his left foot, lifts his right fist above his head (2), steps with his right foot and tries to strike with his fist from above to the top of tori's head (3). He aids his balance by bringing his left hand in a natural position slightly forward.

Tori adjusts his steps to match uke's attack. He can quicken his pace or even stop for a moment to time his own movement correctly.

Tori comes towards uke's strike by stepping on his left foot in front of uke (3). He reacts only at the last moment when uke is unable to cancel the strike. At the same time tori leans backwards, lowers his left shoulder slightly downwards and reaches his left hand deep into uke's hip and around his waist. (4, 5). Tori does not take hold with his left hand from uke's belt but keeps his fingers outstretched on the belt (7).

Tori puts his shoulder into uke's armpit. The shoulder has two functions: it blocks uke's strike and it acts as a fulcrum for the throw.

With his right hand tori takes a grip on uke's left sleeve at about the forearm. At the same time he does tai-sabaki with his right foot and brings his feet in line with uke's feet (6). The angle is about 45 degrees to the kata axis. During the tai-sabaki tori pulls uke's body with his hands into closer contact with his hip straightens his left leg and lifts uke with his shoulder. It is important that tori does not push his hip into uke but pulls uke into himself.

When uke is in contact with tori's left hip tori rotates his whole body in a quick movement to the right and throws uke (6-10). The throw is fast and uke has no time to defend himself. The place of the throw is approximately in the middle of the tatami and the optimum throwing direction is towards the right rear corner of the kata area.

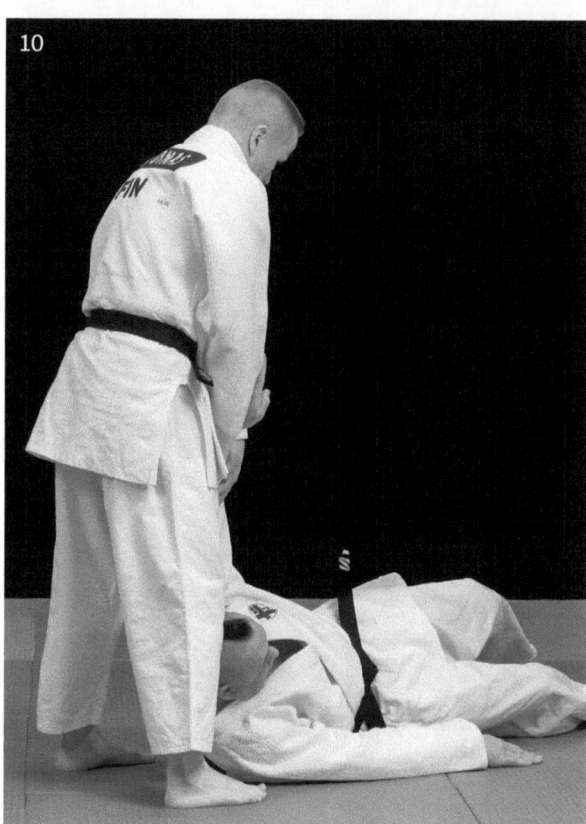

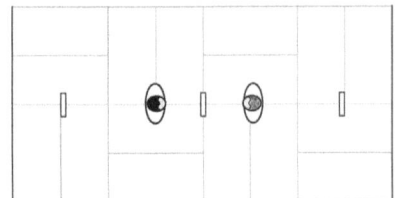

Tori moves to the left of the shomen to the same place as in the hidari-seoi-nage and waits for uke. Uke stands up from ukemi, moves to the right of shomen and at a striking distance from tori. Uke pauses for a moment and then goes to hit tori with his left hand in the same way as before. Tori throws a migi-uki-goshi.

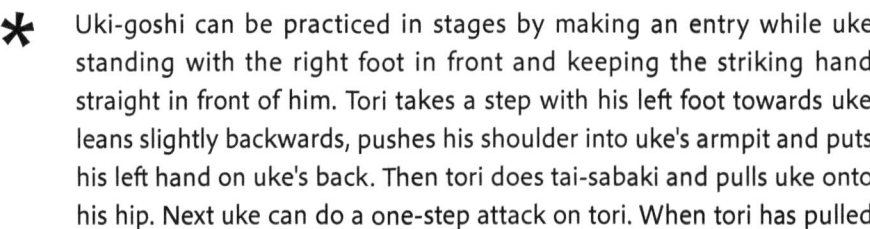

! Tori has to get his shoulder under uke's armpit and lift him and at the same time pull uke against his hip (11). This creates a "floating hip", where uke first comes towards tori and then rolls around the hip. If tori pushes his hip to uke, the throw easily becomes an o-goshi. The most optimal throwing direction is where uke's toes are pointing. If the direction is something else the technique has not gone quite right. This may be because, for example, tori's feet are not aligned with uke's feet, or because tori's hip technique has deficiencies.

* Uki-goshi can be practiced in stages by making an entry while uke standing with the right foot in front and keeping the striking hand straight in front of him. Tori takes a step with his left foot towards uke, leans slightly backwards, pushes his shoulder into uke's armpit and puts his left hand on uke's back. Then tori does tai-sabaki and pulls uke onto his hip. Next uke can do a one-step attack on tori. When tori has pulled uke into contact, he uses his shoulder to lift uke into the air (12-14).

11

Instead of a strike, a similar movement can be practised in a situation where uke is pushing his hand towards tori's neck. This can be followed by a free movement throwing practice.

HARAI-GOSHI Harai-goshi in nage-no-kata is almost in its original form. For the novice judoka, the most difficult part of the throw is perhaps the execution of the throw standing only on one foot. Harai-goshi is well suited as one of the first kata throws to learn, as it is relatively easy to perform.

PRINCIPLE

The principle of tori is to break uke's balance to the front right and take hip contact with uke's lower abdomen. This allows tori to throw uke by 'pushing' with his right leg uke's right leg upwards and roll uke over tori's hip.

TEACHING

Harai-goshi teaches kuzushi from a backward tai-sabaki where tori has first brought uke closer. It also teaches throwing when standing on one foot and the importance of the correct use of the hands for an effective throw.

KUZUSHI

Kuzushi is made to the front right looking from uke.

IMPORTANT

The throw must be made from a proper kuzushi.

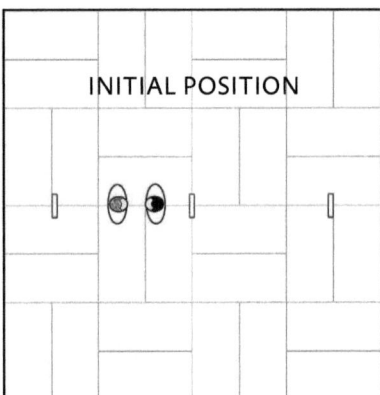
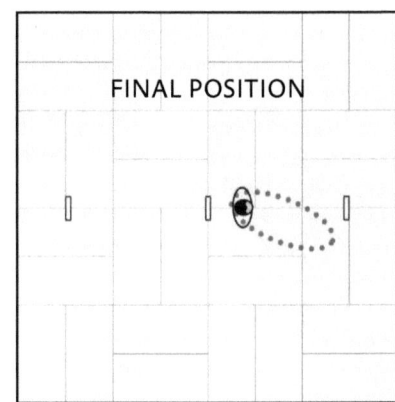

EXECUTION

After the uki-goshi tori moves to the same position from where the uki-otoshi started and waits for uke. Uke stands up from ukemi and comes to within about 60 cm of tori. Tori is on the right and uke on the left.

Uke tries to grip tori in migi-shizentai in the same way as in uki-otoshi and kata-guruma. Tori reacts and moves backwards before uke has got a grip. Both take tsugi-ashi step and tori has the initiative (1).

Tori takes another tsugi-ashi step backwards and puts his right hand under uke's left armpit to his back (2). Right palm comes over uke's shoulder blade and the fingers point upwards (3). In order to get his hand on uke's back, this step can be a little shorter than the first step. Tori must not bend his body forward or twist his upper body too much to reach uke's back better. During the movement, tori uses his body to pull Uke along and tries to break his balance forward. Uke tries to maintain his balance and steps a tsugi-ashi forward. Because tori's hand is on uke's back the distance between the pair is now smaller and uke is more off balance forward.

Tori takes a short step backwards with his left foot and steps behind his right foot and turns his body to the left (4). Tori's toes are almost pointing in the direction of the movement and his right side is towards uke. While turning tori pulls uke forward with both hands and forces uke to step forward with his right foot. The direction of the pull is first forward and then slightly diagonally to the right looking from uke. As a result of tori's kuzushi uke is forced to also step forward with his left foot almost to the same level with his right foot (5). At the same time uke's foot comes a little closer to his right foot. When uke keeps his body taut, the left foot moves naturally. Tori has now broken uke's balance forward and slightly to the right and uke's weight is more on his right foot. Tori pulls uke closer and puts his hip firmly against uke's lower abdomen. When unbalancing is done correctly, uke's heels come off the mat (5, 6).

Tori starts the sweep with his right leg guiding with his hands to the front right looking from uke and rolls uke around his hip (7-9). When uke is lifted off the mat, the hand on uke's back continues to push, tori's forearm is in contact to uke's body and the sleeve hand guides the throw in the right direction. Uke's body is guided as if to pass tori. The hand on uke's back is particularly important and tori needs to have good hip contact with uke's body before the sweep. The sweep of the leg must not be exaggerated and the throw is made with minimum force. Tori keeps the sweeping leg almost straight and the ankle outstretched. The sweep is slightly outward and not straight backwards. The throwing position is slightly off the centre line to the direction of advance.

9

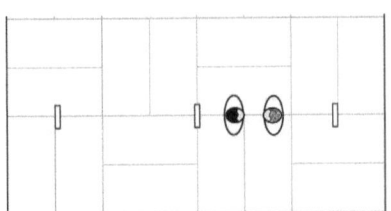

Tori moves to the starting position of the hidari throw and waits for uke. Uke stands up from ukemi and comes to stand in front of tori. Uke starts to take grip in hidari-shizentai and they start the left harai-goshi in the same way as before.

! Tori has to break uke's balance in a manner that he does not pull uke directly into his lap. The correct direction is slightly to the front right of uke. Very important for a successful throw is the correct use of the hip. It must be in contact with uke and the throw is made over the hip (7). When kuzushi and contact are good the role of the leg is simply to act as a barrier to prevent uke from going around the throw.

Uke's role is to stay straight without bending or twisting his body in any direction.

✱ Harai-goshi training should start with a single step and only with tai-sabaki (10, 11). Next perform tai-sabaki by bringing uke into hip contact (12, 13). The third step is to bring the sweeping leg in.

A similar backward tai-sabaki can be used in free movement for other similar throws such as hane-goshi, uchi-mata, ashi-guruma and o-guruma.

When practising harai-goshi, the movements can be very calm and a technically clean throw can still be made.

TSURIKOMI-GOSHI The principle of tsurikomi-goshi in nage-no-kata differs from that in randori. The focus in kata is to study the blocking of the throw and a continuation to that block. The throw requires from tori strong leg and body muscles and mobile shoulder joints. Young people may have difficulty controlling the motor skills required. If done incorrectly there is a potential risk of injuring the shoulder.

In the original tsurikomi-goshi kata version, tori first attempted a higher hip throw, but uke blocked it, prompting tori to lower his position and throw uke. Nowadays, uke does block the supposed throw, but tori goes straight for the tsurikomi-goshi.

PRINCIPLE
The principle of tori is to first break uke's balance forward when uke's feet are parallel. Tori does this by pulling and lifting. Then tori falls uke over the low support point.

TEACHING
Tsurikomi-goshi teaches how to make tai-sabaki forward from a backward movement. It also teaches going into a deep squat, kuzushi and lifting over a fulcrum in a situation where uke's defence position is weak forward.

KUZUSHI
Kuzushi is done simultaneously with tai-sabaki, going down and lifting and pulling.

IMPORTANT
Kuzushi must be maintained during the tai-sabaki and going down.

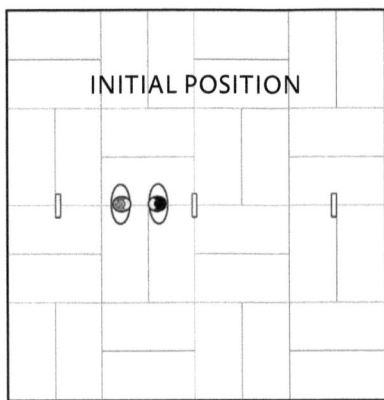
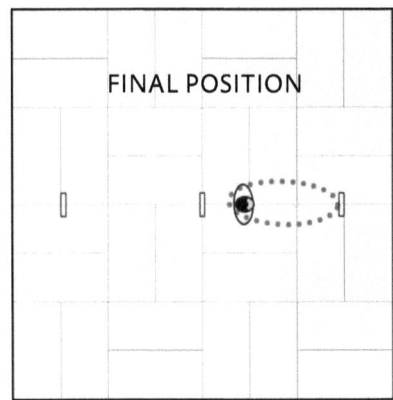

EXECUTION

After harai-goshi tori moves to the same position where the uki-otoshi began and waits for uke. Uke stands up from ukemi and comes about 60 cm from tori.

In the same way as in the uki-otoshi, uke tries to grip tori in migi-shizentai. Tori reacts to this and moves backwards before uke has the grip (1). The difference to other techniques is that tori takes the right hand grip directly to the collar at uke's neck (2). This is the only throw of the nage-no-kata where the grip is this deep at the neck. Uke's grip is normal. Both take a tsugi-ashi step, and tori takes the initiative.

Tori takes another tsugi-ashi step of the same length backwards in an attempt to break uke's balance forward. Uke tries to maintain his balance and takes a tsugi-ashi step forward (3). The situation has not changed much from the first step. Uke's balance is still slightly worse than that of tori. Tori steps with his left foot the third step backwards. This step is longer than the previous steps. Immediately after this, tori brings his right foot half way between his own left foot and uke's right foot and pulls uke forward (4). Uke steps forward with his right foot, reacts and starts to counter the kuzushi by stepping with his left foot alongside his right foot and straightening his upper body. Both uke's heels are on the tatami (4, 5).

Tori turns his body to the left and brings his left foot next to his right foot. The right hand both pushes up and pulls forward, and the left hand should not yet have too much pull. Tori bends his knees, lowers his hips to the level of uke's thighs and draws uke against himself. Tori must go down during the turn so that he comes past uke's hands. When going down, tori must not push uke back to balance, but the pulling and lifting must continue all the time. Tori's back must be straight and the right arm is almost or completely straight. Tori's stance must be firm.

Uke is still trying to stay upright by keeping his back straight. Due to tori's kuzushi and uke's straightening body, uke's heels come off the mat (6). Tori throws uke straight forward by pulling down with both hands and straightening both legs in a quick motion. Tori in a way "tips" uke over him and pulls down with his hands (7-10). The throw is performed approximately in the middle of the kata area or slightly in the direction of advance.

9

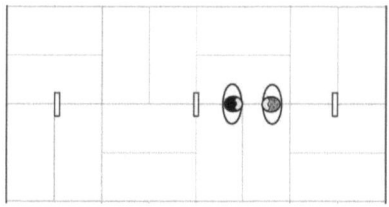

Tori moves to the starting position of the hidari throw and waits for uke. Uke stands up from ukemi and comes to the right side in front of tori. Uke tries to grip tori in hidari shizentai and they start on the left side tsurikomi-goshi in the same way as before.

10

! Tori performs tai-sabaki in tsurikomi-goshi with the right foot stepping forward. Sometimes tori has been taught to make tai-sabaki by turning straight with his left foot backwards. In this case, however, the elements of the throw are more difficult to demonstrate.

When throwing, uke's block with the heels on the mat, tori's entry going down and simultaneous making kuzushi and uke's fall over the hip all must be made visible. The absence of kuzushi can be seen by the fact that uke's heels do not come off the mat during the entry. The lack of tipping is shown by the fact that uke goes clearly first upwards and then into ukemi during the throw without leaning forward.

In the past it has been taught that uke blocks with the back arched and the hips in front. This exaggeration has since been discontinued.

✱ Tori can practise correct positioning with both standing and uke is behind the back of tori. Uke raises his arms up, and tori grabs uke's sleeves with both hands (11). Tori lowers down and pulls uke onto his back. Tori must go down so that tori's buttocks hit the thighs just above uke's knees. Tori straightens his legs and lifts uke up (12).

Then tori and uke stand facing each other and tori crosses his hand and takes a grip of uke by the sleeves (13). When turning to the migi side, the left hand is above the right hand. Tori makes a forward tai-sabaki and the same movements as above. Tori can slowly pull uke over him in which case uke does a handstand and a slow somersault (14, 15).

Next tori and uke practice the third step of tsurikomi-goshi and tori lifts uke to his back. This can be followed by a single step throw and finally all three steps.

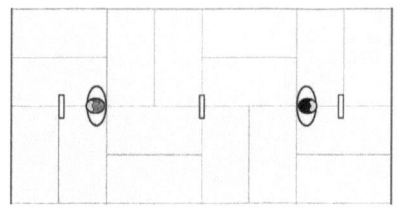

ADJUSTING THE JUDOGI

After the left tsurikomi-goshi is performed, both return to their places after the opening step at a distance of about four metres from each other. Tori and uke have their backs towards the centre and adjust their judogis.

Ashi-waza

A student of Jigoro Kano once asked him which ashi-waza throw he learned first. Kano replied de-ashi-harai, ko-soto-gari and sasae-tsurikomi-ashi, all together. When he was asked for the clarification on this he said that when he studied kitō-ryū and tenjin shin'yō-ryū jujutsu a situation often arose in randori where the opponent had bad balance. This made it easy to sweep the foot and throw him. This was also done by his teachers. Gradually, however, Kano began to wonder whether there was a principle behind it all that he could exploit. He considered a situation where uke changed his weight from one foot to the other. If at that very moment tori sweeps or stops the leg from moving, it's easy to do kuzushi and the throw is relatively simple to execute. Kano said that this principle was the first time he understood the meaning of tsukuri. In jujutsu, no one had realised this before. All ashi-waza throws in nage-no-kata demonstrate this insight.

2. Sasae-tsurikomi-ashi

Ashi-waza includes OKURI-ASHI-HARAI (1), SASAE-TSURIKOMI-ASHI (2) and UCHI-MATA (3).

1. Okuri-ashi-harai

3. Uchi-mata

OKURI-ASHI-HARAI The okuri-ashi-harai is the only throw of the nage-no-kata in which movement is done along the lateral kata axis. In the past, the throw was also performed along the longitudinal kata axis. Tori moved to uke's side and the couple set off with tori's backs to the shomen. This can also be done nowadays, if there is too little space in the direction of the throw. Another option on a small tatami is to come closer to the shomen at the beginning and start from there.

Okuri-ashi-harai is a demanding throw that requires accuracy in motor skills and especially control of the lower body. The practice of the throw is usually preceded by the practice of de-ashi-harai.

PRINCIPLE
Tori brings uke into an accelerated lateral movement and times the sweep precisely at the moment when uke's both feet are off the tatami.

TEACHING
Okuri-ashi-harai teaches lateral movement with tsugi-ashi together with uke and to follow the rhythm of uke. It also teaches utilizing rapid sideways movement in the throw and the correct timing of the sweep.

KUZUSHI
Kuzushi is based on the movement that is just before the sweep slightly intensified with the hands.

IMPORTANT
The sweep must be timed just right.

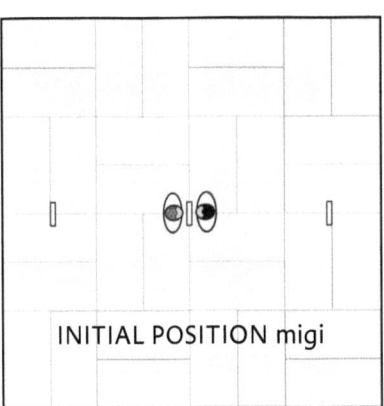

INITIAL POSITION migi

FINAL POSITION

EXECUTION

After adjusting the judogi tori and uke move to face each other in the middle of the tatami. They stop in shizen-hontai about 30 cm apart (1).

While standing in the shizen-hontai uke tries to grip tori. Since the distance is smaller than in other throws, uke does not have to take a small step forward. However, tori is faster and starting with his right foot, steps straight sideways to the right and takes a grip. Tori should take a left hand grip more from the side of the sleeve allowing tori to use his hand to effectively steer uke. Uke does not want to lose his balance to his side and takes the grip and steps to the side with his left foot (3). During the

first side step tori is pressing lightly on uke's elbow towards uke's body and controls uke's movement.

Tori's left hand pushes horizontally (2) as he completes tsugi-ashi by bringing his left foot close to his right, without fully joining them. Uke responds and brings his right foot close to his left foot (4). This first sideways tsugi-ashi is slow and the movement almost stops. The movement sideways is performed smoothly without bouncing up and down. The heads move in a straight horizontal line. It's easier to do this by bending the knees a bit and lowering the centre of gravity slightly. Movement proceeds directly away from shomen.

Tori takes another tsugi-ashi in the same direction to the side, adding speed and power to the movement. Tori's left hand guides uke to move and controls uke's movement. Uke doesn't want to lose his balance and follows tori (5).

Tori takes the third step with his right foot to the side while pushing uke lightly with both hands in the direction of movement and slightly upwards. The third step is faster and longer than the second step and the speed increases. Tori can turn the toes of his right foot slightly to the direction of the movement. Uke steps with his left foot to the side and follows tori (6). Just as uke starts to bring his right foot close to his left foot tori turns the sole of his left foot and starts to sweep towards uke's right ankle (7).

Tori will time the sweep to the exact moment when uke's weight is shifting from one foot to the other and uke is at his highest point (8). The sweep comes at uke's ankle bone and tori concentrates his power on the outer edge of the sole of his left foot. Simultaneously with the sweep tori pushes uke's elbow with his left hand towards uke's body and in an arc slightly upwards. With his right hand tori lifts uke. The movement of the hands are intended to lighten uke and reduce the friction between uke's feet and the mat.

Tori must do the sweep so that uke's both feet remain parallel. Uke's tsugi-ashi must be normal. The sweep is not very long. Tori throws uke in the direction of the movement. In ukemi uke's head stays roughly at the feet of tori (10, 11). The place depends, among other things, on the speed of the lateral movement. The throw is made low, so that uke almost falls on the spot as the legs are swept out from under him.

Tori remains standing at the throwing position waiting for uke. Uke stands up from the ukemi and moves to stand in front of tori. Tori is on the right and uke on the left. Then uke takes a hidari grip in shizentai. Tori responds and they begin to perform a left okuri-ashi-harai moving towards the shomen.

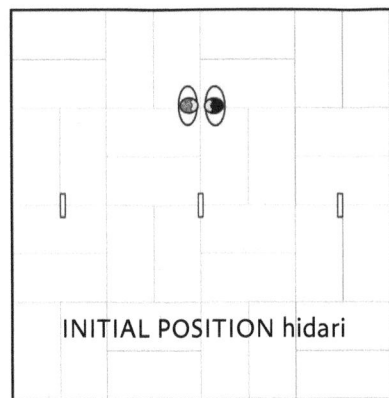

INITIAL POSITION hidari

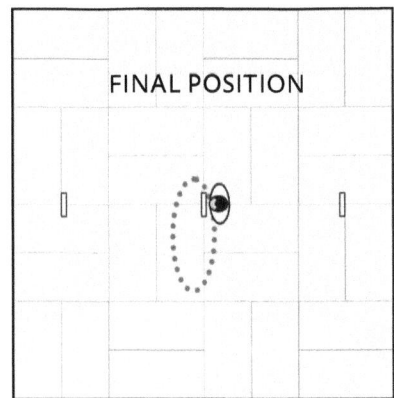

FINAL POSITION

! In the sideways movement, the knees should be slightly bent so that the centre of gravity moves vertically as little as possible. Bouncing can be easily seen, for example, in the movement of the head.

In okuri-ashi-harai, it is important that both feet are swept. Otherwise the throw will be either de-ashi-harai or harai-tsurikomi-ashi. A bad sweep is often caused by uke when he moves his right foot forward or backward during his last step.

Acceleration of movement speed is also very important. If the speed is not fast enough uke's feet will not rise into the air at the same time. This is often connected with uke jumping when he is thrown.

Okuri-ashi-harai has also been made so that uke actively started moving to the left and pushed tori to move with him. Tori took advantage of uke's movement and threw him. Nowadays tori takes the initiative right after uke's attempt to grip.

Sometimes it has also been taught that tori pushes uke strongly with his hands to the side throughout the movement. However, this is not the model taught today. A throw with a strong push by tori is recognised by the fact that the throw becomes high and uke lands quite far even with a slow movement. A similar ukemi can be seen when uke jumps.

✳ Okuri-ashi-harai should be practised in stages and at slower speeds. As your skills improve, you can increase the speed.

At first, just practice with the bouncing uke on the timing of the throw. First, uke bounces high and then continuously lowers the height of the bounce. Tori tries to hit uke's foot at the right moment (12). Then side steps can be taken and only the movement of the arms without throwing uke. Next, the sweeping foot is lifted to uke's ankle, but still not throwing. Finally, the whole sequence is performed. These movements can be used as a warm-up.

SASAE-TSURIKOMI-ASHI

It has been said that "judo should begin and end with ashi-waza". De-ashi-harai, sasae-tsurikomi-ashi and hiza-guruma are still included in the Kodokan gokyo-no-waza in the first group of throws to be taught. Previously these three throws were in many countries a requirement in the yellow belt examination. Perhaps the idea was that judoka should learn them from the very beginning because these throws take so long to learn.

The difficulty of the sasae-tsurikomi-ashi is that tori's shoulders rotate in a different direction than the hips. The hands and foot form the contact surfaces and they are far apart. It is difficult to get sufficient power for the throw, and good body control is required. Throwing also requires uke to have the courage to make a straight forward rolling ukemi without support from tori's body or his leg. Sasae-tsurikomi-ashi has remained the same in the kata since the beginning.

PRINCIPLE

By increasing the distance, tori creates a situation where uke has to take a third step. Tori takes advantage of this and stops uke's forward coming foot while it's still in the air and throws uke.

TEACHING

Sasae-tsurikomi-ashi teaches how to do kuzushi by changing the step pattern and retreating further away from uke. It also teaches how to use the whole body by rotating the shoulders and hips in different directions. At the same time it teaches how to use the pulling hand (hiki-te) and the lifting hand (tsuri-te) for the throw and the correct timing of the throw.

KUZUSHI

Kuzushi is performed by increasing distance and with body movement that is intensified with the hands.

IMPORTANT

Tori must stop uke's advancing foot.

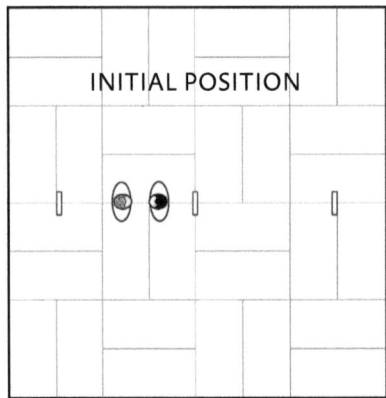
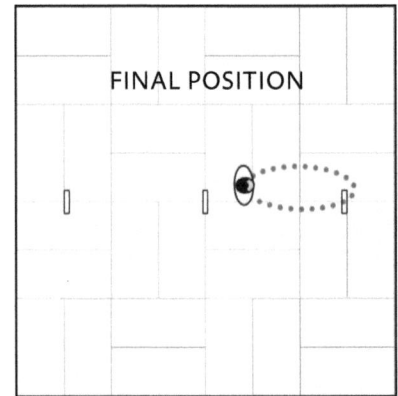

EXECUTION

After okuri-ashi-harai, tori moves to the same position where the uki-otoshi began. Uke stands up from ukemi and moves to the front of tori about 60 cm from him.

In the same way as in uki-otoshi and kata-guruma uke tries to grip tori in migi-shizentai. Tori reacts to this and moves backwards before uke gets his grip. Both take a tsugi-ashi step and tori takes the initiative (1, 2).

Tori takes another step with his left foot backwards. Uke tries to keep his balance and takes a step forward with his right foot (3).

Tori starts to bring his right foot back along the same line as before as if to take a tsugi-ashi step. Uke completes his own tsugi-ashi step with his left foot. However, tori does not stop his foot to the front of his left foot but continues to move the foot past his left foot and takes it diagonally backwards to the right on tatami (4). At the same time he turns his right foot inwards, turns his body to the left and shifts his weight onto his right foot. The movement of tori's foot to the side starts only when the feet are almost adjacent. Depending on the size difference between tori and uke the place of tori's left foot may vary. Due to step to the side and increased distance and tori's turning he has made kuzushi. Tori increases the power of the kuzushi by pulling diagonally slightly

upwards with his left hand and by slightly pushing uke upwards with his right hand (5). Uke doesn't recognize tori's retreat in time and tries to maintain his balance by moving his right foot forward (5, 6). Uke tries to take all steps in the same length. When uke's advancing foot is approximately at the same level as tori's supporting leg tori turns the sole of his left foot and puts the sole just above uke's ankle and stops uke's advancing foot (6, 7). Tori continues a

strong pull with his left hand, lifts with his right hand, twists his upper body strongly to the left and throws uke (8, 9). At the beginning of the throw the hips and legs are tense against the rotation of the upper body. During the throw the pulling direction of the arms changes to downward and tori uses his hands to help uke to make a proper ukemi. During the throw uke's weight causes tori to turn in the direction of the throw.

It should be noted that since the step of tori's supporting leg is to the side, after the throw tori is no longer on the kata axis. Uke makes ukemi straight ahead but pulled by tori he lands slightly to the side from the kata axis.

Tori moves to the starting position of the hidari throw and waits for uke. Uke stands up from ukemi, moves to the right of tori and faces him. Then uke starts to take a grip of tori in hidari-shizentai which tori reacts to and they start a hidari-sasae-tsurikomi-ashi in the same way as before.

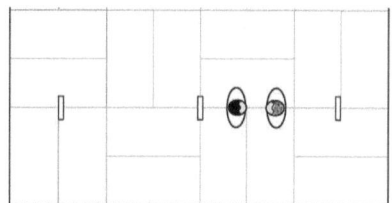

9

! Tori must create distance and give space to ukemi by stepping sufficiently to the side and slightly back. If tori steps directly to the side or even towards uke kuzushi will easily fall short and the throw will be made with force almost using only the hands.

Sometimes it is also taught to make the throw at a moment when uke's foot is already on the ground. Sasae-tsurikomi-ashi can also be performed when the foot is on the ground, but the kata focuses on Kano's principle and to the moment when the weight is shifting to the advancing foot.

In kata competitions, the sasae-tsurikomi-ashi is thrown in the manner described above, with tori rotating on his right foot (10, 11). On other occasions it is possible for tori to take step forward with the left foot

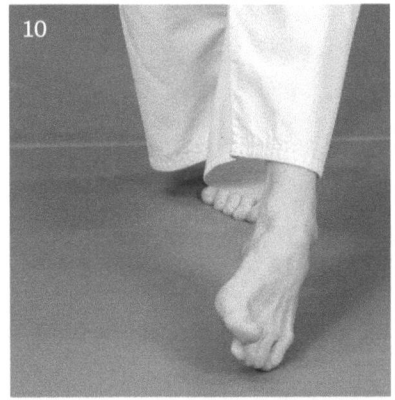
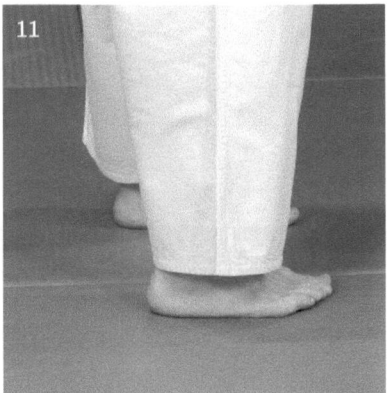
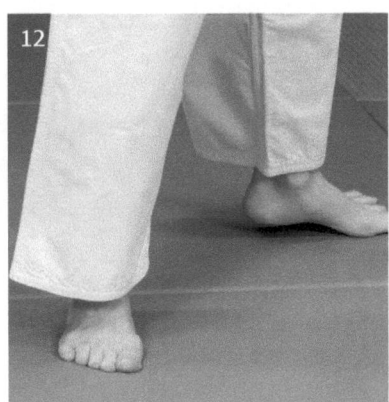
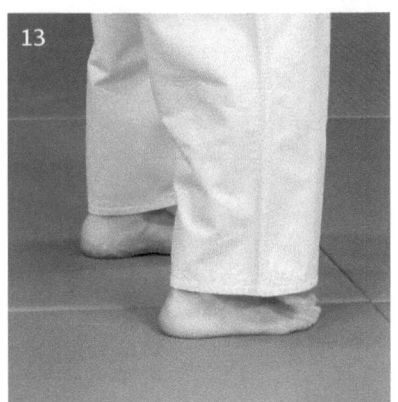

at the end of the throw (12) and bring the right foot alongside it (13). This makes the throw easier, especially for pairs of different sizes.

 The movement of the throw can be practised as uchi-komi with tori holding the ends of the belt in his hands and uke holding the centre of the belt (14). This is done in one step and finally in the right movement. Tori must make the correct movements with arms and legs and keep the body straight and the hips in front.

    The movement can be practised with a partner from one step. Tori takes a step with the right foot back to the side, releases the grip and lets uke do ukemi freely (15, 16). This can be continued with tori also making kuzushi with his hands and letting go (17, 18). As an intermediate step uke can kneel down and tori makes the throwing motion and uke makes a low ukemi. The next step is to throw in one step.

UCHI-MATA   Uchi-mata can be a difficult throw for some people, as it requires tori to control the balance together with uke when standing on one supporting leg. The additional difficulty comes from the fact that in nage-no-kata the uchi-mata is done as an ashi-waza throw and lacks the supporting hip contact. Especially when done on the weaker side uchi-mata is one of the most difficult throws in nage-no-kata for many.

Earlier uchi-mata was done with a high collar grip. Nowadays the basic grip is taken. There have been variations also in starting distances.

PRINCIPLE

Tori uses centrifugal force in the throw. He moves in the inner circle and uke in the outer circle giving uke greater speed and putting him on his toes. The second principle is to time the throw to the moment when uke is about to transfer his weight to his advancing foot.

TEACHING

Uchi-mata teaches the meaning of the pulling hand and the lifting hand in rotational movement and tsukuri in this situation. It also teaches kuzushi, the correct timing of the throw and the throw standing on one foot.

KUZUSHI

Kuzushi arises from the rotational movement, and tori intensifies it at the final step by pulling uke with the hands towards himself.

IMPORTANT

Tori must continue the movement of uke's leg just as uke's weight is shifting to the left foot.

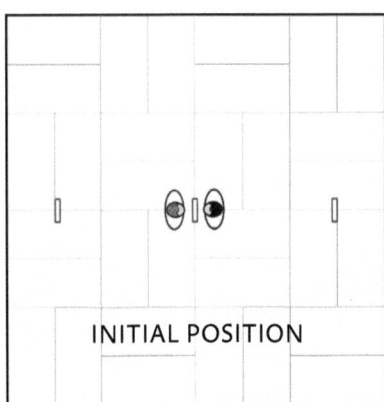

INITIAL POSITION

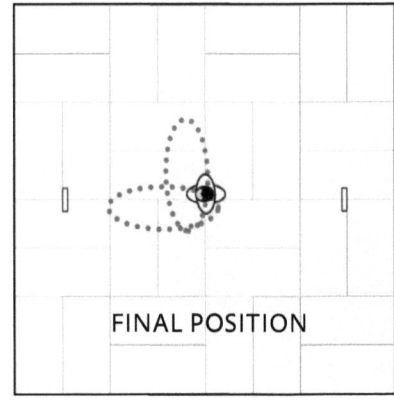

FINAL POSITION

EXECUTION

After hidari-sasae-tsurikomi-ashi tori moves to the right of the centre line and waits for uke. Uke gets up from ukemi and comes to the right of tori at a distance of 60 cm and faces tori. Both stand at equal distance from the centre line.

Uke steps forward with his right foot half a step and takes a grip of tori. Almost simultaneously, tori also takes a half step forward with his right foot and takes a grip of uke. Both are in migi-shizentai (1).

Tori steps with his left foot diagonally to the left at about the same level as uke's right foot and pulls with his right hand uke to the right behind him. Tori's pull is horizontally to the side. When pulling, tori's hand is slightly hooked. Tori ends the first tsugi-ashi by bringing his right foot close to his left foot. Uke responds to tori's move and steps first with his left, then his right foot to the side (2–4). Due to the pull of tori's hands tori's right side is now almost towards uke. Neither brings his feet together in tsugi-ashi.

Tori takes another step with his left foot and continues to pull with his right hand (5). This step is diagonally to the front and closer to the centre of the rotational movement than the first. Tori finishes the tsugi-ashi with his right foot (6). During the steps, tori's side is towards uke's belt knot. Uke tries to keep his balance and responds to tori's move by stepping forward with his left foot (5, 6) and then with his right foot (7). Uke's steps are similar and as far from the centre as the first. As uke moves on a larger circumference than tori, his lateral speed is greater than that of tori.

Tori takes a short step forward with his left foot and pulls uke in a wide arc to the right and behind him (7, 8). This third step is shorter and more central than the previous ones. Initially the pull is to the side but changes to a pull towards tori. However, tori does not pull uke into a tight contact with his upper body. Uke tries to retain his balance and takes another step to the side as before and stays on the outside circle. Due to the kuzushi uke's weight shifts to his toes and he leans forward (9).

At this point the heel of tori's supporting leg should be on tatami and the knee slightly bent. Just when uke's left foot is touching the tatami and his weight is shifting to this foot, tori brings his right leg between uke's legs, bends his left knee, leans his body forward and sweeps uke's left inner thigh with his right hind thigh up and outwards (10, 11). Tori sweeps with his leg backwards, not sideways. At the end of the throw tori turns naturally a little to the left to support uke.

Uchi-mata is done standing fairly straight. Tori does not lift the sweeping leg very high or lower his head very low (11). Approximately horizontal leg and upper body is sufficient. Minimum force is used to achieve maximum power. During the throw, uke is lifted up approximately horizontal and then he will be rotated longitudinally around tori's leg and falls down almost laying across transversely in front of tori (13).

One model of tori's and uke's steps is shown in the drawings. The steps proceed in numerical order. Each pair has to use the steps that suit them the best. For example, size difference affects the length of the steps, the amount of rotation and where uke lands.

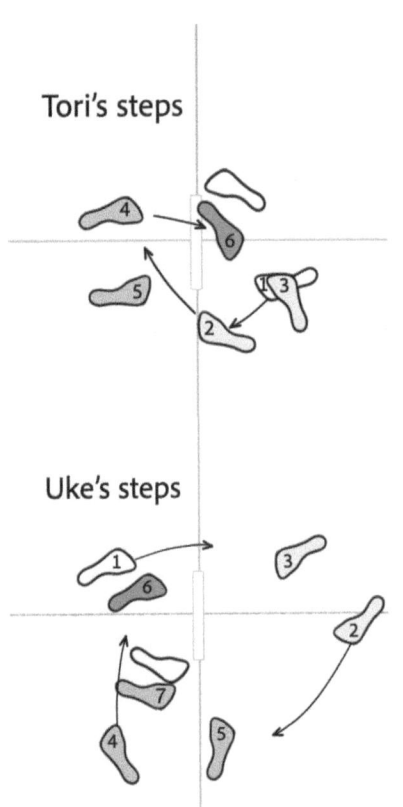

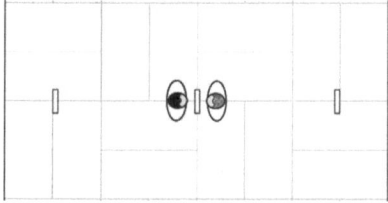

Tori moves to the left of the centre line and waits for uke. Uke stands up from the ukemi and walks to the right in front of tori. Tori and uke take a grip in hidari-shizentai and start the left uchi-mata in the same way as before.

! An essential element for a good uchi-mata is to do the rotation in a natural way and continue from there to kuzushi. Tori should be slightly ahead of uke at all times and continue the movement before uke has regained his balance after uke's tsugi-ashi steps. By observing uke's position and his feet, one can see how well tori succeeds in this. If the pull of tori's hands is too strong and in the wrong direction the rotation becomes angular and it becomes difficult to throw.

Uke's landing place can vary greatly. Uke's legs may be parallel to the kata axis, away from the shomen, or something in between. The important thing is to get enough rotation to make the throw, and to get into the correct throwing position. Once kuzushi is done correctly and the timing is right, uchi-mata is easy to do.

In Nage-no-kata, uchi-mata is presented as a leg throw, with tori utilizing uke's weight shift from one foot to the other. If uke is loaded on the hip, and the throw is made as a hip-uchi-mata, the technique is not is no longer a leg throw.

Uchi-mata can also be performed in kata with similar timing as okuri-ashi-harai. It is where tori waits for uke to come to bring his right foot next to his left foot. This is not really an error, but when executed in this way the throw does not fully correspond to the principle.

Practicing uchi-mata can be started with a tandoku-renshu by doing both the role of tori and uke on the circumference of the circle. The next step is to practise with a partner, choosing a 1 x 1 m area. Tori tries to go around inside the circle and pull uke inside. Uke tries to stay outside the circle (14).

After this, only the last step is practised. Tori steps forward and pulls uke towards him and uke tries to turn around further around the circle. No throw is made but tori lifts his foot to a contact with uke's inner thigh. Next the same is done in three steps and still without the throw. The aim is to get kuzushi and timing to work. Finally, uchi-mata is done with the throw.

ADJUSTING THE JUDOGIS

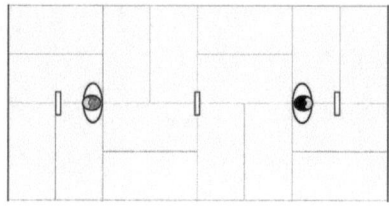

After the left hand throw, tori and uke go to adjust their judogis about four metres apart. If uchi-mata is the last throw of the kata to be performed, tori and uke turn towards each other after the adjustment of judogi, take the closing step and start closing (see closing formalities) the kata.

14

Ma-sutemi-waza

The first introduction to sacrifice throws for a judoka is most often tani-otoshi. It is a simple and easy to understand technique.

In all sutemi-waza (ma-sutemi-waza and yoko-sutemi-waza) the common principle is to utilize one's own body weight for the throw. The throw cannot be performed with the hands alone or by lifting uke with tori's foot.

Of the sutemi-waza throws, uke performs ukemi by coming up to standing position except for two throws (ura-nage and yoko-gake). The old masters criticized that when the sutemi throw is done properly uke cannot stand up in ukemi. However, for the safety of uke tori releases his grip and lets uke make a proper ukemi. The principle used in the throw has been shown already earlier.

In ma-sutemi-waza, tori ends up lying on his back after the throw. Kodokan lists only five throws to be included in this group. All of the throws presented in nage-no-kata are effective in randori and competition.

The throws of ma-sutemi-waza are TOMOE-NAGE (1), URA-NAGE (2) and SUMI-GAESHI (3).

1. Tomoe-nage

2. Ura-nage

3. Sumi-gaeshi

TOMOE-NAGE Tomoe-nage is a throw familiar also to those unfamiliar with judo from films and TV series. Although it may seem easy it is technically difficult. When failed, it also involves a risk of injury.

Tomoe-nage in nage-no-kata is a typical example of a throw based on the use of uke's reaction. In kata it is almost in its original form. Only the number of steps was initially undefined.

PRINCIPLE
Tori exploits the situation where uke corrects his position by moving forward. Tori continues uke's movement forwards and upwards and makes a throw sacrificing himself backwards.

TEACHING
Tomoe-nage teaches tori to feel uke's opposing force when he pushes uke backwards. It also teaches tori to time the change of direction, kuzushi and the start of the throw to the moment when uke makes the counter-move. For uke, it teaches how to make an ukemi longitudinally over tori.

KUZUSHI
Kuzushi is done when uke has stepped forward but has not yet regained his balance.

IMPORTANT
The start of the sacrifice must be timed just right.

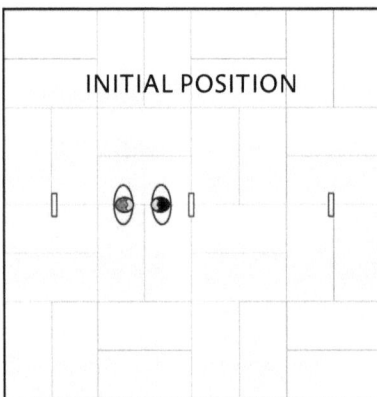

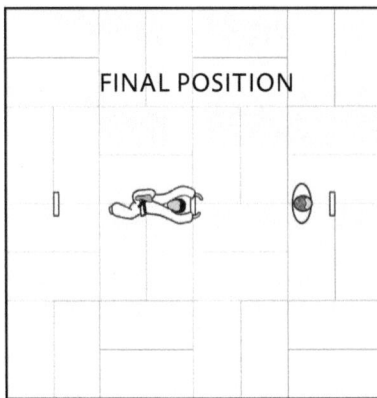

EXECUTION

After adjusting judogis tori walks to uke and uke comes slightly towards tori. They stop facing each other about 60 cm apart. The place is one metre from the centre line and a little closer to the centre than in the uki-otoshi (1).

Uke takes a small step with his right foot and tries to take grip of tori in migi-shizentai. Tori responds and takes a step with his right foot and takes grip of uke in migi-shizentai (2).

Tori steps forward with his right foot and starts to push uke backwards (2). He takes three ayumi-ashi steps at a fairly fast pace forward. The steps are of normal length. Uke resists the push but retreats backwards first left, then right, then left foot. After his third step, uke pushes and tries to regain his balance (4). The counter push should not be exaggerated by a backwards leaning position, but uke's back should be in a relatively vertical position.

When uke resists more strongly tori stops the push. To correct his balance uke straightens up and takes a step with his left foot forward (5) and brings it alongside with his right foot. As uke's foot starts to move tori moves his left foot to the side of his right foot and brings his left arm under uke's armpit to his right lapel (6). Tori's feet are now between uke's feet and the tips of their toes are almost in line. The exact

position depends on the size difference between tori and uke. During the movement, tori has squatted down about a head height and the forearms are almost vertical (7). Too upright, or too low squatting position can make sacrifice difficult. Before uke has properly regained his balance in shizentai tori makes kuzushi by pulling uke diagonally upwards with both hands and leaning backwards. As a result of tori's kuzushi uke's heels come off the mat (6).

Tori immediately begins to sacrifice himself and when uke's left foot has become alongside the right foot tori places the ball his right foot on uke's lower abdomen (8). The knee of the lifted leg should be in line with tori's body and not pointing to the side. Tomoe-nage is a sacrifice throw and it should be visible. The place where tori lands on his back on the mat depends on the size of the pair and must be mutually found. If tori sits close to his own heel the throw will easily become cramped. If tori stays too far away, the fulcrum is not under uke's centre of gravity and the throw is difficult to make.

Tori throws uke over his head by pulling with both hands and straightening his right leg (9-12). Movement of the hands form an arc. The foot does not kick at any point.

Tori keeps the ball of his left foot on the tatami and his right foot upright. Hands are pointing in the direction of the throw. Tori's eyes do not follow uke. Tori guides the throw and releases his grip at the moment when uke can make a safe ukemi.

Uke tries to stop the throw by stepping with his right foot to tori's left side but is unable to prevent the throw (10). Uke brings his right hand to the front for the ukemi, does not jump and does the ukemi just naturally to the place where tori throws him. Uke makes ukemi by coming up to a standing position.

Tori stands up and moves to the starting position of the hidari throw. Uke comes to the front of tori at a suitable distance. Then tori and uke take their grips in hidari-shizentai and start the hidari-tomoe-nage in the same way as before.

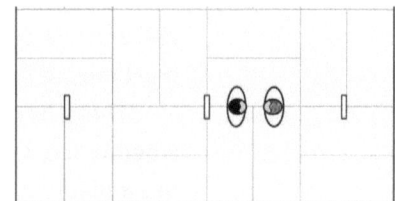

! The purpose of the initial steps in tomoe-nage is to provoke a reaction from uke to the push. . Therefore, walking as a form of stepping should not be commonly agreed. Tori must push and uke begins to resist the push. The forces must be real, but not exaggerated. Tori must be able to utilize uke's movement forward in making kuzushi. The lack of kuzushi can be seen if uke's heels are still on tatami when sacrificing starts. However, uke shall not lift his heels by himself. The sacrifice must also be real and fast, so that tori uses his body weight in an effective manner. Tori must release his grip at the right time so that uke can make a safe ukemi.

There have been different interpretations of uke's corrective step whether it is a reaction to the end of tori's push, or whether tori is pulling uke and forcing him to take a step. It is currently taught that uke takes the step himself to correct his balance. The end result with these interpretations have no bearing on the outcome, because tori has to make kuzushi just before uke regains his balance.

✳ Tomoe-nage can be taught together with sumi-gaeshi and uki-waza, as the preparation and methods of the throws are similar, with ukemi performed over tori in all three. Throwing principles and kuzushi differ clearly from each other.

Ukemi over tori can be practiced with tori lying on his back, placing a foot on uke's abdomen. Uke steps forward with the right foot near tori's side and performs a free ukemi, placing a hand near tori's left shoulder, then stands up (13–14).

The second exercise can be done from the moment when kuzushi is started. Tori's feet are almost together, the knees are slightly bent and the hands are on uke's lapel. Tori's forearms are upright against uke's chest and tori will unbalance uke on to his toes. This can also be done as an uchi-komi from uke's corrective step forward on. Then tori starts to sacrifice without lifting the foot on uke's abdomen. Uke makes a free ukemi (15-18).

After this the throw can be practised. It is important that first tori starts to sacrifice and only then puts his foot on uke's stomach.

URA-NAGE Ura-nage begins with uke's strike attack. It may look like the harshest throw in nage-no-kata although ukemi in yoko-gake often falls harder than in ura-nage. Ura-nage carries a risk of injury if tori and uke do not dare to do their part properly. Once the throw has been started, it be cannot be stopped.

Ura-nage has its roots in jujutsu techniques. In the original nage-no-kata version tori went much more to uke's side so that the hand on the back went farther. Today the approach is more directly from the front.

Principle
Tori takes advantage of uke's forward movement by coming towards the strike and getting under uke's centre of gravity. Tori guides uke's motion energy further up and forward.

Teaching
Ura-nage teaches tori to dodge uke's strike by going into contact with uke and to use uke's motion energy for the kuzushi and the throw. It also teaches the correct timing of the throw and the correct use of the feet and the muscles of the whole body to lift uke. Ura-nage teaches uke a harsh ukemi.

Kuzushi
Tori does kuzushi by pulling with the left arm around uke's waist uke against tori's body and leaning backwards.

Important
Use of hands and the whole body when lifting and starting the throw.

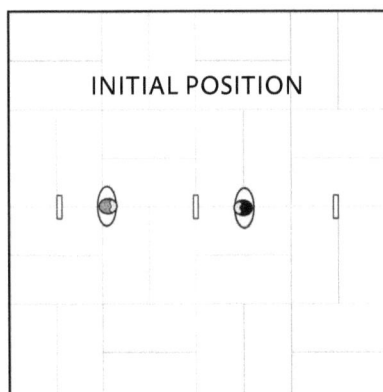
INITIAL POSITION

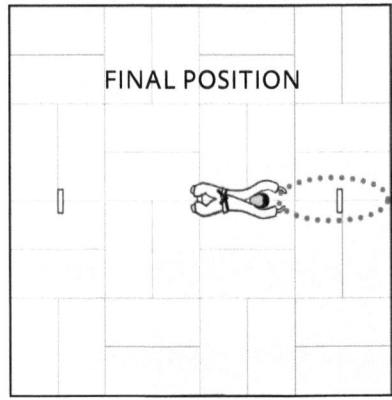
FINAL POSITION

EXECUTION

Immediately after the hidari-tomoe-nage, tori and uke stand up, turn around, and move toward each other. Uke approaches tori at a fairly fast pace but not running.

When they are about two metres apart, uke starts his attack and strikes towards the top of tori's head. The approach and the start of the attack should be practised so that the throw will be done roughly in the centre of the mat.

If necessary, tori stops and waits for uke. Uke steps forward with his left foot, raises his right fist above his head (1), takes a step with his right foot, and strikes.

Tori comes against the strike by stepping his left foot outside uke's right foot and crouching down at the same time (2). He encircles his left hand deep around uke's waist along uke's belt and immediately brings his right foot between uke's feet and in line with his left foot (3-5). Tori's chest is facing uke at all times. Tori's left hand does not take grip, but the fingers are straight and together at uke's belt. Tori steps in one foot at a time and he lowers himself under uke's centre of gravity. The exact position of tori's feet depends on the size difference between tori and uke. Usually, tori's feet are shoulder-width apart and slightly overlapping in depth with uke's feet.

Tori pulls uke to a tighter upper body contact with his left arm and presses his face against uke's chest (5). If there is no contact, the lift will be difficult to do. Tori places the palm of his right hand on uke's belt knot or slightly to the right of the knot (4). Tori's fingers point upwards. Tori makes kuzushi by keeping his hands in tight control with uke, lifting up with the hands and feet and by leaning backwards with his body (6).

After tori dodges uke's strike, uke's striking hand goes far onto tori's back. Uke can take support with his left hand by placing his palm on tori's right shoulder or his hand in v-shape on uke's elbow bend (6). This will also help uke to keep the throw in a straighter line. After kuzushi, uke's feet become parallel but apart. When tori performs the lift, uke must remain in a natural position and not twist his upper body to the left.

Tori lifts with his arms and legs, throws himself backwards and throws uke over his left shoulder (7, 8). During the throw, tori lands on both shoulders on the mat (9). The direction of the throw is straight along the kata axis. Uke's trajectory is first upwards and then more horizontally downwards.

At the end of the throw, tori's shoulders and the soles of the feet are on tatami. Tori's back is arched and the arms are outstretched. Tori does not follow uke with his gaze.

Uke does ukemi staying on the mat.

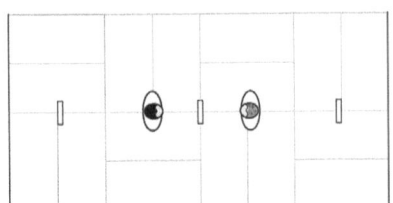

Tori stands up and moves to the starting position of the hidari throw, which is about a metre on the left side of the centreline. Uke stands up and moves to within striking distance of tori, stops and then starts his attack with a left-handed strike.

! In all katas where uke attacks tori in any way tori must wait until the attack is so far advanced that uke can no longer change his attack to another attack. This is also the case in the ura-nage. The couple must find the right moment so that the technique looks natural and tori does not have to wait for the strike to progress.

In the past it was taught in some countries that the ura-nage was based purely on uke losing his balance when his strike did not find the target. Nowadays it is required that there is also kuzushi in the throw.

Uke must remain straight in the throw and allow the throw to come over tori. If uke goes into ukemi clearly sideways, it becomes more difficult to make ukemi.

If age or health conditions prevent a full speed throw and a hard ukemi, ura-nage can be made more softly by first making kuzushi and then landing in a squatting position on your back. Tori then uses his hands to guide uke into a ukemi over himself (10, 11). In this case uke should press his striking arm against tori's back and keep it there. The arm is pulled out from under tori at the very end of the ukemi.

✱ Ura-nage training should start moderately. In the first phase, tori is squatting and uke is standing in front of tori with his hands up. Uke takes a step forward with his right foot and makes a slow strike. Tori wraps his left arm behind uke's back and brings his right palm on uke's belt knot (10). Tori starts to fall backwards, and uke makes a ukemi straight over tori (11).

In the second step, both start from standing position and do the same in two steps. Tori squats down in front of uke and lets uke do ukemi over him. In the third stage tori takes a tighter contact, makes kuzushi and a soft throw by crouching and going on his back. Tori should learn how to pull uke's body into contact before the throw. Only when tori has learned how to pull uke into contact with himself tori brings in his right hand into the knot of uke's belt, fingers upwards. The hand in the belt knot acts like a foot in a tomoe-nage.

After this, you can move on to practising the harder throw. The difficulty with ura-nage training is that the real throw cannot be practised at half speed. The role of uke is important here. Uke must have the courage to strike with enough power and to go for ukemi properly.

SUMI-GAESHI Sumi-gaeshi is another throw in the nage-no-kata performed from the jigotai stance. Although the throw may seem simple, it involves many elements that are demanding in terms of motor skills and timing.

Sumi-gaeshi is a technique of the old jujutsu schools. In the original version of sumi-gaeshi, the positions of the supporting leg and the throwing leg were slightly different than today, but otherwise the throw has retained the original shape of the throw.

PRINCIPLE

Tori uses the pull of his arms, the movement of his body and his positioning to get uke to react exactly in the way he wants to create the optimum throwing position. Tori's first movement forces uke to take a corrective step with his right foot to regain his balance. When uke attempts a corrective step tori is faster and causes uke to lose his balance forward. Sumi-gaeshi also applies the principle that uke with his legs apart has less resisting force than tori with his feet together.

TEACHING

Sumi-gaeshi teaches jigotai and how to move in it. It also teaches how tori uses uke's opposing force by changing direction. In addition, it teaches the control of one's own centre of gravity in relation to uke's centre of gravity.

KUZUSHI

Kuzushi is done with body movement and simultaneous lifting and pulling with the hands and pulling uke towards tori.

IMPORTANT

Timing of the initiation of kuzushi and sacrifice.

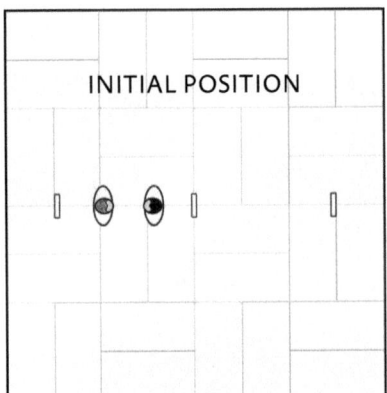

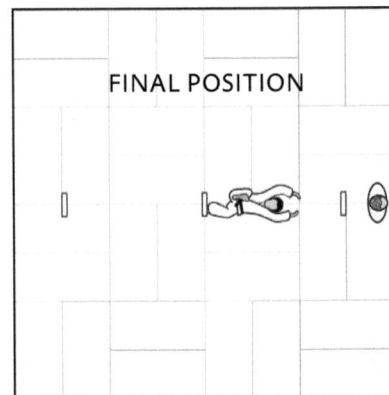

EXECUTION

After ura-nage tori moves a little less than one metre to the left of the centre line. Uke stands up and moves to the front of tori at a distance of 90 cm from tori (1). Uke starts to take a grip in the migi-jigotai position. Tori reacts immediately and takes the grip in jigotai at the same time as uke. In jigotai tori takes his right hand under uke's left armpit on uke's back. The fingers point slightly upwards. Tori's left hand is the palm open beneath uke's upper arm. There is no grip on uke's sleeve. Knees are bent and the head is next to uke's head. Heads do not touch each other. Upper body is tilted slightly forward and the back is straight (2). Uke's posture is similar to tori's.

Tori starts to break uke's balance by lifting and pulling with his right hand and stepping back with his right foot in an arc of about 90 degrees (2-4). Uke tries to keep his balance and takes a step forward with his left foot (5). During the step tori uses his hands to guide uke to the direction of the movement. The force comes from the twist of tori's body and not from the movement of the arms. Uke begins to resist tori's movement. Tori's hands control uke with a lift and also with a slight pull towards himself. Uke's weight is now more on his left foot (5). Both are still in the jigotai position and the bodies are facing each other.

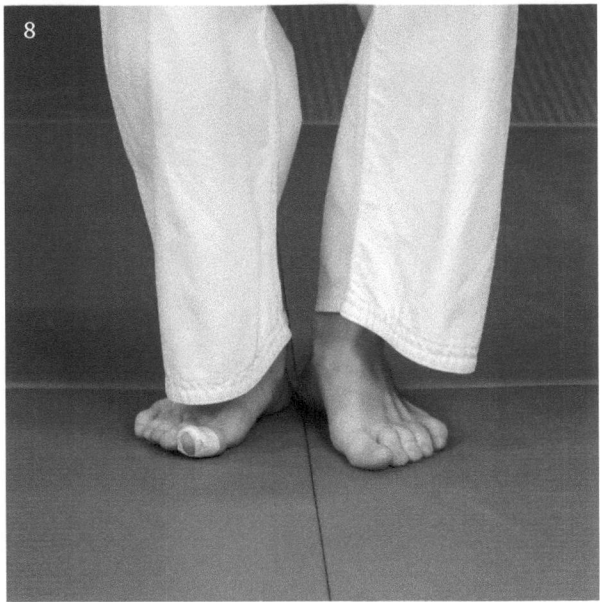

When tori's right foot comes to the ground tori stops twisting his body and the push to the right. As the force disappears uke's resistance is reduced and his body straightens slightly. Uke's movement is not very large. Tori's and uke's heads are still side by side. Tori continues to lift uke up and towards him. Due to the pull and the lift uke is in danger of losing his balance. Uke starts to take a step with his right foot in the direction of tori's pull which is towards the right front corner of the kata area (6).

At the same time as uke starts his right foot step tori takes a step backwards with his left foot and turns his side towards the shomen (7, 8). Due to tori's movement the direction of uke's step becomes parallel to the kata axis. Tori keeps his arms slightly bent and uke still close to him.

Uke brings his right foot to the tatami to the same level with his left foot (8). Both tori's and uke's sides are now facing the shomen. Just as uke's right foot hits the tatami and before uke regains balance tori lifts up and forward with both hands and starts the kuzushi. Uke tries to resist and keeps his weight back but cannot avoid tori's kuzushi resulting uke's heels coming off the mat (9). Up to this point, the heads are almost side by side.

Tori starts to sacrifice straight backwards, pulls upwards with both hands with force and keeps his knees bent. Tori holds uke close to him at all times. When the effect of the sacrifice is obvious tori raises his right ankle, hooked, to the inner thigh of uke's left leg just above the knee bend (9-11). Tori sits close to the heel of his left foot. Uke takes a step forward with his right foot to the left side of tori.

Tori throws uke over his head by lifting his right foot and by lifting and pulling with both hands (12–14).

Uke makes a ukemi over tori's upper arm without removing his arm from tori's armpit. Uke turns his right hand to ukemi position during the throw (12, 13).

At the end phase of the throw, tori releases his grip of uke and lets him do the ukemi. At the end of the throw, tori's left foot is on the mat, hips are off the mat, right leg is upright and arms are outstretched. Tori's gaze does not follow uke. The direction of the throw is directly along the kata axis. (14). Uke makes ukemi by coming up to a standing position.

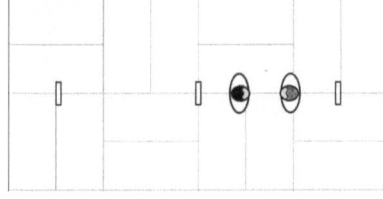

Tori stands up and moves to the right of the centre line to the starting position of the hidari throw. Uke comes to a suitable distance in front of tori. Both take a grip in jigotai and they start the left sumi-gaeshi in the same way as before.

! The first movement of the sumi-gaeshi can be explained, for example, so that tori first tries to throw uke with a kind of uki-otoshi towards the right back corner (15, 16).

It is important that the steps and forces used to prepare the throw are real and not a an agreed upon sequence of actions. Uke must not take the second step until he is forced to do so. When the preliminary steps and kuzushi are done correctly, uke has lost his balance going forward and the throw continues naturally. Uke does not have to jump into ukemi. If uke jumps it can be seen as a straightening of either the leg or the ankle before the ukemi.

To ensure that tori catches uke's leg with him tori must bend his ankle up into the hook.

Sumi-gaeshi has been done in the past also in a way that uke strongly resists tori's pull of the first step and straightens up. From this tori has continued by bringing his left foot alongside his right foot, by performing kuzushi in an almost upright position, forcing uke to take a corrective step and then starting to sacrifice. This is quite different from the way it is taught today where the forces are smaller and the heads do not rise much above the original jigotai. There has also been variation in the amount of contact and depth of the crouch in jigotai posture.

✱ Sumi-gaeshi can be practised starting from a low position. Tori lies on his back and uke is standing between his legs. Tori lifts his right ankle up to the knee bend of uke's left leg. Uke takes a step with his right foot and does an ukemi over tori's left shoulder. No grip is taken (17, 18).

In the second phase, tori and uke are in the throwing position and tori has his feet between uke's feet. Tori starts to sit down with his back straight. Uke is unable to resist and becomes slowly off balance. Tori is merely using his own weight to pull uke. Uke takes a step forward and makes ukemi over tori's left shoulder.

Once tori has understood the use of his own weight in the throw he can start using preparatory steps and throw uke.

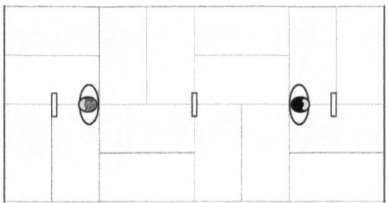

ADJUSTING THE JUDOGI
After the left hand throw, tori and uke go to adjust their judogis at a distance of about four metres from each other. Then they turn towards each other and begin the yoko-sutemi-waza.

1

YOKO-SUTEMI-WAZA

The name of this group refers to the fact that when the throw is finished tori is on his side.

There are many more yoko-sutemi-waza throws in the Kodokan technique catalogue than ma-sutemi-waza throws. This is understandable since there are many more directions of movement where tori will end up on his side than where tori ends up on his back.

Many of the sacrifice throws inherit from the old jujutsu (koryū) techniques. In these schools, the randori was done in a jigotai position with one hand on the opponent's armpit. In Kodokan randori was done in the shizentai position. At the time of the development of the nage-no-kata the sacrifice throws done from shizentai were still being finalised. Perhaps this is the reason why the nage-no-kata still has two throws that need to be done in jigotai position.

Yoko-sutemi-waza throws include YOKO-GAKE (1), YOKO-GURUMA (2) and UKI-WAZA (3). The reason for the choice of yoko-gake to nage-no-kata is uncertain. It is known that in the past it was a popular randori and competition technique. One reason for this is thought to be judogi, where the sleeves and trouser legs were short. When the sleeve could not be gripped you could get a strong grip on the inside of the sleeve, which allowed you to get close to your opponent and enabling a strong kuzushi. Another reason may have been that the old tatami had much lower friction compared to the modern tatami. Back then it was easier to make sweeping leg throws like the yoko-gake.

1. Yoko-gake

2. Yoko-guruma

3. Uki-waza

YOKO-GAKE A yoko-gake is a harsh throw for an uke when done correctly. It doesn't have anything for uke to get support from during the ukemi because tori also is in the air. In addition uke falls on his back. It is a throw where kuzushi, tsukuri and kake are particularly difficult.

In the original version tori took a full third step with his left foot but left his right foot in place. The throw was made far from uke and almost directly from the front. Today, tori brings his supporting leg close to the sweeping leg.

PRINCIPLE
Tori breaks uke's balance on uke's right little toe so that uke cannot bring his left foot forward or backwards to get support for himself. Tori makes a sweep at the precise moment when both tori and uke are about to lose their balance.

TEACHING
Yoko-gake teaches tori to break uke's balance onto his front foot. It also teaches a strong gake throw at the moment when both are losing their balance. It teaches a very harsh ukemi to uke.

KUZUSHI
Kuzushi is done with the body and hands forcing uke onto his little toe.

IMPORTANT
The sweep must be timed just at the moment of loss of balance.

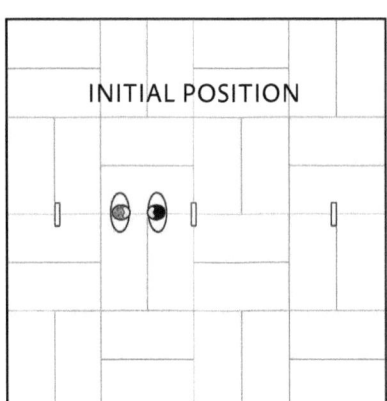

INITIAL POSITION

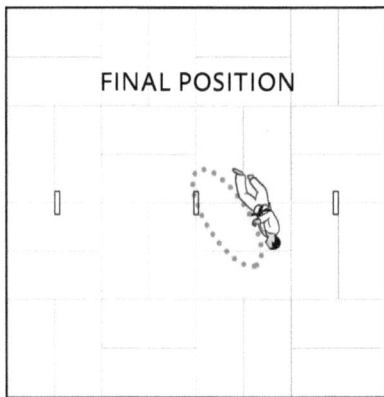

FINAL POSITION

EXECUTION

After adjusting the judogis tori and uke turn simultaneously and move to the same position where uki-otoshi started. The distance between the pair is about 60 cm. In the same way as in uki-otoshi uke tries to take a grip in migi-shizentai. Tori reacts to this and moves backwards before uke can get a grip. Both take a tsugi-ashi step. Tori has taken the initiative at this point and has broken uke's balance slightly forward (1). Tori does not yet turn uke with his hands.

Tori takes another tsugi-ashi backwards with his left foot. This step is a little shorter than the first step. Moving backwards tori forces uke to take a tsugi-ashi with his right foot forward. Uke's step is the same length as the first step bringing him closer to tori. During his step, tori presses with his left hand uke's right elbow inwards and lifts with his right hand on uke's lapel slightly upwards. (2, 3). In this way tori forces uke's body into a slightly tilted position. However, tori must not break uke's balance too much yet.

Tori steps again with his left foot slightly backwards and also moves his right foot a little bit. Uke is now forced to take a third step with his right foot. When uke's foot is on the ground, tori presses hard uke's elbow inwards with his left hand and lifts with his right hand (4). Tori is still waiting for uke to complete his tsugi-ashi and his left foot to come behind uke's right foot. Uke's weight is now on his little toe and his body is in a twisted position to the left. Uke's left foot is off the tatami (5). The direction of the kuzushi is diagonally to the front right from uke. Tori has made the correct kuzushi when uke cannot move his left foot to either to the front or to the back to block the throw. At this point uke should not bend his upper body but must try to stay upright until the very end.

Tori leans heavily backwards to the left and breaks uke's balance further (5). Just when tori or uke are about to fall to the side tori quickly moves his right foot close to uke and pushes strongly the sole of his left foot against uke's right foot (6) and throws himself onto his left side.

The sweep is done by pushing, not kicking, and it touches uke's ankle. The direction of the sweep is in line with uke's legs so that both uke's feet come off the mat.

Tori supports uke's ukemi with his left hand. During the throw tori releases his right hand from uke's lapel and may also use this hand to support uke's right elbow and help uke to make a good ukemi. Tori falls on his side on the tatami and uke falls straight on his back (7, 8). After the throw tori's left side is on the mat, the left leg is straight against the mat and the right knee is slightly bent. Tori's left elbow is on the mat and he is supporting uke with his upright hand. Uke keeps his feet together and does not lift them up too high. After the ukemi, uke lowers his feet on the tatami. Uke's belt is almost on the kata axis at the same place where he was standing before (9).

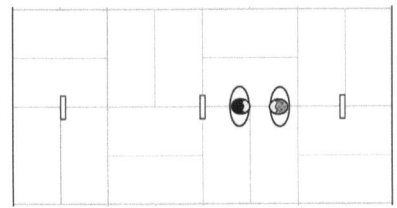

Tori and uke stand up at the same time. Tori moves to the starting position of the hidari throw and uke comes to a suitable distance from tori. Then they take a grip in hidari-shizentai and start the left yoko-gake in the same way as before.

! Yoko-gake is based on a strong kuzushi on uke's small toe. Often this kuzushi is incomplete or the direction is wrong. The throw must be timed precisely to the moment of loss of balance. From this situation tori must push both of uke's feet simultaneously with his left foot. The weight of the whole body must be behind the push. Uke must have the courage to do a proper ukemi or the throw will not succeed. A well-made throw is characterised by a relatively slow kuzushi but a quick throw.

If the sweep hits only one foot, the throw becomes de-ashi-harai. For those judokas who, due to age or physical limitations, cannot perform a harsh ukemi, this is a softer alternative. The kuzushi is made the normal way followed by a softer fall to the mat.

For the last step of the right foot the yoko-gake has been taught in many ways in the past. Either a step to the side has been taken or tori has stepped towards the movement. Some of these ways are related to the size difference of the pair. Nowadays it is taught to keep the right foot on its own line and move it closer to uke to a place to which the foot advanced at the end phase of the kuzushi.

* In Yoko-gake it is good to practice ukemi. In the first stage tori holds onto uke's right hand with both hands and moves further away (10). Tori continues to slowly retreat slightly backwards diagonally to the left. Uke keeps his body rigid until he can no longer prevent the fall (11). The direction of the kuzushi is towards the little toe. Uke's gaze is forwards all the time.

In the second step, a belt is wrapped around the ankles of uke. The assistant holds the ends of the belt almost level with the tatami and keeps the belt taut. Tori retreats away and breaks uke's balance almost to the point of tipping over (12). The assistant pulls on the belt, uke does ukemi and tori supports uke standing upright (13). The direction of the kuzushi and the pull on the belt are in the same direction as in the throw itself. The pull should be quite calm, so that it corresponds to a push with the foot.

Tori can practice his own steps as tandoku-renshu. Throwing can be started with the soft version where the gake step is done like in de-ashi-harai.

YOKO-GURUMA

Yoko-guruma is the only throw in nage-no-kata in which uke counters tori's throw and tori continues with another throw. The throw is done very much in the same way as in the original version.

PRINCIPLE

Tori takes advantage of uke's poor balance to the front after uke has blocked tori's first attempt and changes the direction of the throw.

TEACHING

Yoko-guruma teaches how uke can defend against the ura-nage and how tori can continue the situation by changing the throwing direction and technique. It also teaches the correct use of the hands, while tori sacrifices himself underneath uke.

KUZUSHI

Kuzushi is done mainly with the left hand by pushing uke to the tips of his toes.

IMPORTANT

Sliding the foot between uke's legs at the right moment.

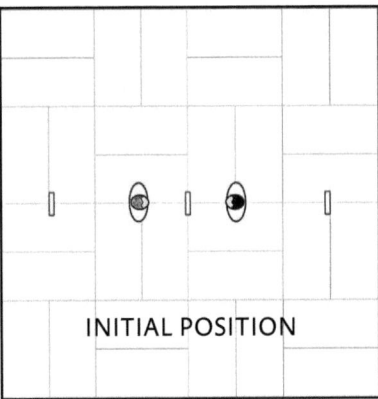

INITIAL POSITION

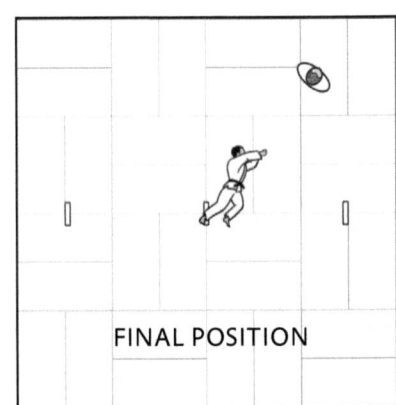

FINAL POSITION

1

EXECUTION

After hidari-yoko-gake, both stand up and they face each other in the middle of the kata area around two metres apart. The starting positions are the same as in seoi-nage.

Uke takes a step forward with his left foot, raises his right fist above his head (1), takes a step with his right foot and tries to hit tori from the top to tori's head (2).

2

Tori comes against the strike by stepping his left foot outside uke's right foot and crouching down at the same time (2, 3). His intention is to throw uke with an ura-nage.

Tori encircles his left hand deep into uke's back along uke's belt and immediately brings his right foot between uke's feet and in line with his left foot (3-5). Tori pulls uke with his left hand into a tighter upper body contact, presses his face against uke's chest and places the palm of his right hand to uke's belt knot or slightly to the right of the knot (4, 5).

Uke sees the ura-nage coming and blocks the throw by quickly bending his upper body forward. Uke's striking hand will be slightly bent and tense and comes forward over tori's shoulders or neck (6). Uke's blocking must be real. Uke must prevent tori from straightening out and throwing him with ura-nage.

During the block uke does not bring his hands together. Tori takes advantage of uke's defensive jigotai position and lifts his left elbow to break uke's balance straight forward towards his toes. Uke's heels come off the mat (6 , 7). Then tori starts to

sacrifice. He slides his right foot deep between uke's legs and controls uke with both of his hands (8). Tori does not put his right foot sole on the mat and does not bounce with his right foot. Uke can no longer move his right foot. Tori keeps uke close to him until the effect of the sacrifice is obvious. Tori uses his right hand to push uke over his left shoulder, and left hand pull rotates uke around his longitudinal axis. Tori must be able to loosen the control of his hands in time to let uke do ukemi properly. When too much force of the hands is involved it will be difficult for uke to come up to a standing position from the ukemi.

Tori will throw uke over his left shoulder and turns his body to his left side (9, 10). The direction of the throw is towards the direction of uke's toes. This is roughly at about 45 degrees angle to the left from the direction of travel.

At the end of the throw tori lies on his side, with his back arched, hips off the mat, arms outstretched and gaze following uke (10).

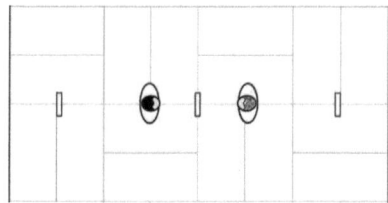

Tori stands up and moves to the left of the shomen about one metre from the centre line. Uke walks to the right of the shomen within striking distance of tori. After a moment he starts to attack with a left hand strike. Tori does a hidari-yoko-guruma.

! When throwing with yoko-guruma tori must first attempt to throw with ura-nage which is followed by a block from uke. Tori must also clearly break uke's balance on uke's toes before he starts to make the sacrifice. The absence of kuzushi can be seen if uke's heels remain on the mat until the beginning of ukemi. After the strike is blocked, uke's front is almost towards the back corner. The best throwing direction is towards uke's toes. From the places where tori and uke end up after the throw you can tell if everything went right.

In the past, it has been taught that during the block uke puts his hands together and presses down. At the same time, uke has stepped one step backwards with his left foot. Nowadays it is sufficient for uke to bend forward. The throw was also made with the right leg bent, foot sole on the mat and the left leg was straight. This is how yoko-guruma is done in a technique video of Kodokan throws. But the important thing is that ura-nage is actually blocked and tori continues with yoko-guruma in the direction where uke's balance is the weakest.

✱ Yoko-guruma can be practised in a similar way to sumi-gaeshi from the moment of blocking. From this position tori slides his foot between uke's legs and does the throw with light hand control. The throw cannot be done very slowly because uke cannot move his right foot. The movement of tori's right foot can be practised by placing an object behind uke which tori then tries to push further away with his foot.

UKI-WAZA
Uki-waza was originally the second throw of the yoko-sutemi-waza. It has remained almost unchanged from the beginning. It is a typical example of redirecting uke's resisting force to another direction when uke is trying to correct his position.

PRINCIPLE
Tori's first step places uke in a situation where he is forced to start the corrective step with his right foot and then tori changes the direction of the pulling force. The second principle is, like in uki-otoshi, to surprise uke by extending the pull and going down so that uke can no longer block the throw.

TEACHING
Uki-waza teaches tori and uke to move in jigotai and how tori can utilize uke's opposing power by changing the direction of the force in a slightly different manner than in sumi-gaeshi. It also teaches the use of body movement and weight in a sacrifice throw.

KUZUSHI
Final kuzushi is done at the end to the front right from uke.

IMPORTANT
Hand and body movement to use uke's reaction and change of direction.

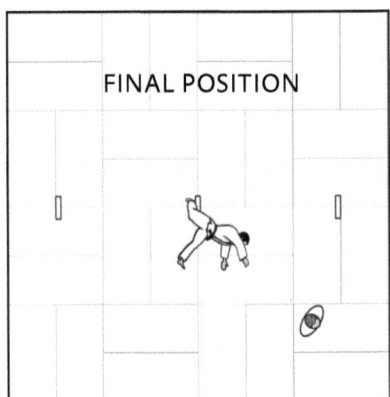

INITIAL POSITION

FINAL POSITION

EXECUTION

After hidari-yoko-guruma tori stands up and moves to the same place where sumi-gaeshi started. Uke stands up and comes to the front of tori about 90 cm from tori (1).

Uke starts to take grip in migi-jigotai position. Tori reacts immediately and takes the grip in jigotai at the same time as uke. The jigotai is similar to sumi-gaeshi (2).

Tori's first movement is similar to the first in sumi-gaeshi. Tori unbalances uke with his right hand lift and pull and steps with his right foot in an arc backwards about 90 degrees (3, 4). The difference

from sumi-gaeshi is that the step is taken farther from the centreline and slightly longer. Uke takes a step with his left foot and tries to maintain his balance (5). During his step tori uses his hands to guide uke in the direction of the movement. The force comes from the turning of tori's body and not from the movement of the arms. At the same time tori's hands lift and hold control of uke with a slight pull towards tori. Uke resists tori's movement. Both maintain the jigotai position the whole time with the bodies facing each other. Because in uki-waza tori's step is further away than in sumi-gaeshi tori puts slightly more pressure on uke's left foot. Hence, uke's weight is more on the left foot and uke's counter-reaction is a little bigger.

When tori's step comes to the ground he stops the turning of his body and the push to the side. As a result of this uke's body straightens out. When tori feels that uke starts to correct his position he changes the direction of his kuzushi and starts breaking uke's balance with both hands up and forward towards himself (6). Uke attempts to regain his balance and moves his right foot diagonally forward (7).

As uke starts to step with his right foot tori further changes the direction of the pull by pulling strongly past his own left shoulder towards the right front corner of the kata area and forces uke to continue his foot movement (8). The change of direction of tori's pull must be a smooth broad-arc movement. At the same time tori starts to sacrifice. He continues his pull looking from uke to the front right, opens

his left leg straight to the side and slides it along the tatami. Uke brings his right foot to the inside of tori's left leg as he is unable to step over it (9, 10). Uke's foot should be on the mat before tori's leg (10). Tori sacrifices onto his left side, continues the pull with his hands, keeps his left leg extended to the side and throws uke (11, 12).

At the end of the throw, tori releases his grip to allow uke to make ukemi. The direction of the throw is about 30–40 degrees from the kata axis towards the shomen. At the start of the ukemi uke's hand is under tori's armpit and uke turns his hand to ukemi position (11). Uke does ukemi by standing up and remains standing for a moment in a good position and balance with his back facing tori (13).

In the final position, tori is lying on his left side, body arched, hips off the mat, arms pointing the direction of the throw and eyes on uke (13). Tori remains in this position for the same time as uke is in his place.

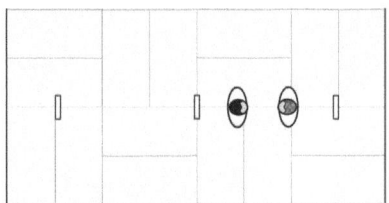

Tori stands up and moves to the starting position of the hidari throw. Uke comes to stand in front of tori at an appropriate distance. Tori and uke take a grip in hidari-jigotai and begin to perform the left uki-waza in the same way as before.

! As in sumi-gaeshi it is important that the steps and forces used to prepare the throw are real and not a an agreed upon sequence of actions. In uki-waza the smooth trajectory of the pull of the hands is essential. When the initial steps and kuzushi are done correctly, uke has lost his balance and the throw continues naturally. Uke does not need to jump into ukemi.

Sometimes it was advised to open the left leg as wide as possible. Nowadays it is sufficient to have the soles of the feet at the same level at the end of the throw.

In the past the throw has also been made in such a way that when tori starts to sacrifice he brings his feet first alongside each other and only then spreads his left leg out to the side. The move may look good but it does not promote the throw.

Tori can practice the first step by testing that if uke does not resist with enough force tori will throw uke using a technique similar to uki-otoshi. Uke may do a half-ukemi or at least lose his balance if tori's actions are not correct. When uke resists in the right way tori will take advantage of this and throws uke with an uki-waza.

CLOSING FORMALITIES

ADJUSTING THE JUDOGI

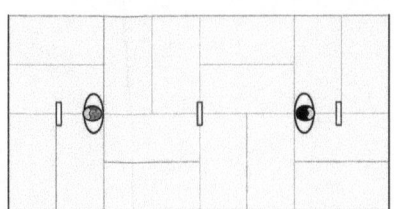

Once the hidari-uki-waza is done tori and uke go about four metres from each other and adjust their judogis with their backs to each other. Then

they turn simultaneously towards each other and take the closing step. After this they descend to the ground and do a kneeling bow.

When they have finished, they stand up, turn to face the shomen and do a standing bow. Finally, they turn towards each other, take backward steps to the edge of the kata area and do a standing bow towards each other.

Nage-no-kata is completed.

固の形

KATAME-NO-KATA

GENERAL Katame in Japanese means to control or dominate. The term katame-waza also includes techniques performed in standing position. These are included, for example, in kime-no-kata and in Kodokan goshin-jutsu. Katame-no-kata includes only the control techniques performed on the mat.

Jigoro Kano developed katame-no-kata slightly after nage-no-kata to supplement the skills needed for mat fighting in randori and competition. Kano included kneeling positions and knee movements to make the kata physically demanding and for strengthening the legs, knees and lower body muscles. For a long time it was also a requirement that uke kept his head off the tatami throughout the kata.

Kano's main focus was on throwing techniques. He developed them much more analytically and thoroughly than katame-waza. However, Kano found that although Kodokan judokas were often superior to those coming from jujutsu schools they were losing matches on the mat. In the 1920s, Kano decided to increase the practice of katame-no-kata in particular in order to improve the skills of mat judo. Kano hired mat judo specialists to Kodokan and kata training was to be held twice a week.

Nage-no-kata and katame-no-kata are, in their basic configuration, completely different. In nage-no-kata, uke starts the initiative which tori turns into his own advantage and makes a throw. In katame-no-kata the techniques are based on a ready arranged situation into which has somehow been ended up. An exception to this setup are the last two techniques which start from a position similar to nage-no-kata situation.

Hon-kesa-gatame.
SOURCE: DJUDO A JAPAN DZSIU-DZSICU,
SASAKI KICHISABURO 1907.

Katame-no-kata is a control kata. The aim of tori is to control uke and to keep the situation as unchanged as possible. Uke, on the other hand, cannot escape unless he can get tori to move. He must try to strike the weak points of tori's control. Tori must be able to counter and control uke by using his whole body and all of his limbs in a holistic way. He does this by following the principle of judo with minimum force, correct positioning of the body and correct timing of movements of the legs and arms to act as support points according to the situation.

By learning katame-no-kata judoka learns the basic principles of mat judo and that mat judo is not just a collection of different twists and individual moves. Uke learns to understand the weaknesses of each technique and to notice when tori reacts late or incorrectly. With each move, uke is actively trying to create new opportunities to turn the situation to his advantage. All these principles can be applied to other areas of mat judo.

In all the techniques of katame-no-kata the same steps alternate: control, weak point, escape attempt, counter. In hold-down techniques this is taken to its furthest extreme when the pattern is repeated three times. In chokes and locks the escape attempts are not always very visible.

In terms of the techniques to be performed, katame-no-kata has retained its form of the early 20th century. The way how katame-no-kata is done has changed significantly. Nowadays, uke makes a serious effort to escape from hold-down techniques and tori really has to fight to block the attempts (1). Previously it has been taught that uke does not really try to escape, nor does he move from his original position. This practice was still common in the early 2000s. For chokes and locks, the change has been more minor.

KATAME-NO-KATA TECHNIQUES

Katame-no-kata has considerably more freedom than nage-no-kata. This is because in the Kodokan kata textbook uke's escapes from hold-down techniques are specified but tori's counter movements are not. Tori can use any counter as long as it is logical, timely and in the right direction. However, the problem for a smooth kata is that uke's next escape is also defined. There are many different and valid versions of tori's counter actions in kata literature. In kata competitions certain ways are preferred because their logic is premeditated.

Katame-no-kata includes three groups of techniques: OSAE-KOMI-WAZA (hold-downs), SHIME-WAZA (chokes) and KANSETSU-WAZA (locks). Each is represented by five selected techniques. Unlike in nage-no-kata the techniques are presented only on the right side in katame-no-kata.

The techniques of katame-no-kata are:

OSAE-KOMI-WAZA
1. Kesa-gatame
2. Kata-gatame
3. Kami-shiho-gatame
4. Yoko-shiho-gatame
5. Kuzure-kami-shiho-gatame

SHIME-WAZA
1. Kata-juji-jime
2. Hadaka-jime
3. Okuri-eri-jime
4. Kataha-jime
5. Gyaku-juji-jime

KANSETSU-WAZA
1. Ude-garami
2. Ude-hishigi-juji-gatame
3. Ude-hishigi-ude-gatame
4. Ude-hishigi-hiza-gatame
5. Ashi-garami

PERFORMING KATAME-NO-KATA

Tori's starting positions are determined by uke's position and it is tori's responsibility to go to the correct place.

During katame-no-kata the back is not turned towards the shomen. However during the execution of some techniques this may happen momentarily. In all hold-down techniques tori always returns uke to the starting position after the technique has been performed. In chokes and arm locks where uke is lying on his back uke may move slightly. If this happens tori may move uke unnoticed to the correct position before returning to his starting place.

When evaluating the kata, attention is also paid to how logical and determined tori's and uke's movements are. Excessive movements which do not contribute to the actual action should be kept to a minimum.

As in nage-no-kata there is no guideline for the duration of katame-no-kata. Typically, katame-no-kata lasts 10–11 minutes.

Tori can calm down the execution of katame-no-kata by waiting for a short moment in the kneeling position before starting the next technique.

IMPORTANT ELEMENTS OF KATAME-NO-KATA

POSITIONS AND DISTANCES

TOMA is a position about 1.2 metres away from uke's body. When tori changes position he always comes first to within toma distance of uke. There are three toma positions. One is on the side of uke and two on the side of uke's head (2-4). The toma on the side aligns approximately with uke's belt. The tomas on the side of uke's head are on the longitudinal kata axis. To one tori goes to when uke is lying on his back and to the other when uke is in a sitting position. In the first two judogi adjustments and in hiza-gatame the toma is in the same place as when uke is lying on his back. Tori moves from toma to toma by walking using ayumi-ashi.

CHIKAMA is a position about 30 cm from uke (5–7). Tori always moves from the toma to the chikama and back with a knee movement. Tori begins and ends, except for the last two techniques, each technique in the chikama. Chikama is explained as a safety distance which ensures that uke cannot surprise tori.

Both toma and chikama are indicative positions. Toma is defined as a half step plus two shikko movements away from uke, while chikama is a half step. Depending on the size of the pair the distance can be adjusted slightly. The most important thing is to keep the chosen distance to uke in the toma and in chikama the same throughout the kata.

In the last two techniques tori and uke together define the appropriate distance.

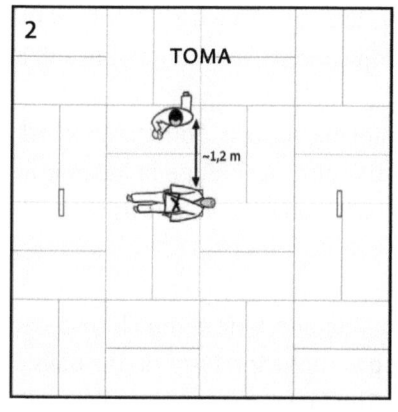

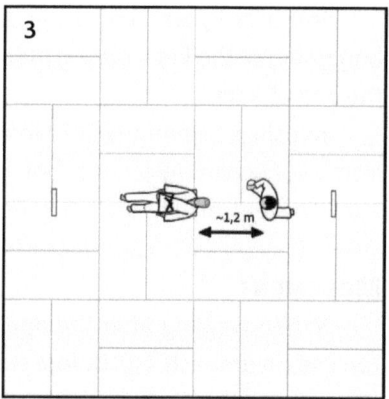

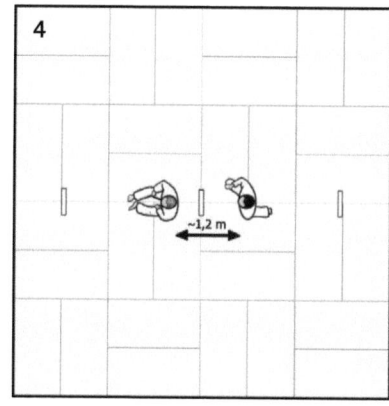

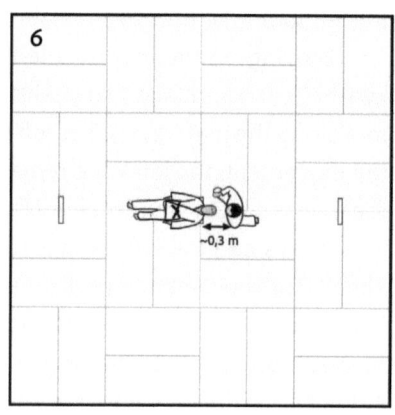

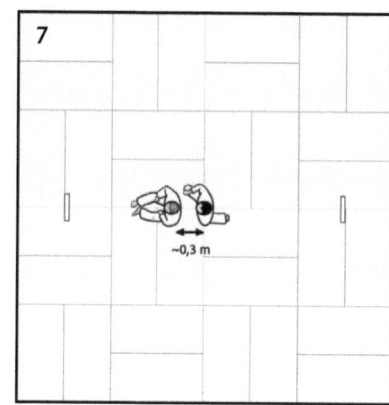

POSTURES

Tori stands up to shizentai when changing from the side of uke's head to uke's side or vice versa. Uke stands in shizentai only after the opening step, at the beginning of the last technique and just before the closing step. When kneeling down to the kneeling position the left knee is put to the same place where the left foot was before.

The kneeling posture is called KYOSHI or KURAI- (8). It is a firm and well-balanced posture in which the left knee and the ball of the left foot is on the mat. The right foot is on the mat, right hand is resting with fingers together on the knee and the left hand is relaxed at the side. The right foot is on the side, the knee angle is 90 degrees with the leg upright and the thigh pointing at about 45 degrees angle to the front right. The toe tips of the left foot are roughly in line with the line of the right thigh. The body is straight and not inclined in any direction. The kyoshi is opened by sliding the right foot straight to the side, keeping the hand on the knee. The position of the upper body does not change. Kyoshi is closed similarly by sliding the foot straight forward. The closed kyoshi is used, for example, when landing down from a shizentai or when standing up from a kneeling position.

Tori uses kyoshi frequently during the kata. Uke uses it only at the beginning of the kata, during judogi adjustments, in hiza-gatame and at the end of kata.

Kyoshi is commonly used in oriental martial arts. Sometimes kyoshi also involves sitting on one foot. This has also been done in katame-no-kata. The kyoshi with the left knee up has been used in kata as well.

MOVEMENT

When walking after the opening step and before the closing step tori uses ayumi-ashi (9). Before starting to move tori turns on the balls of the feet into the direction he is going. The first step is always taken with the left foot. Uke uses ayumi-ashi only in bowings when changing place.

Moving on the mat is called SHIKKO. In the shikko step you close kyoshi (10, 11) and take a step with the right foot by sliding the sole of the foot along the mat (12, 13). The left knee is then brought in behind. During the movement, the left knee remains close to the mat and the ball of the foot is in contact with the tatami (14). The right hand remains on the knee at all times and the left hand is relaxed at the side. The gaze is straight ahead. The movement is performed with the same principle forward and backward (18-21). The step ends to a closed kyoshi. If two steps are taken, the second step follows the first one without stopping in between (10-18). At the end of the movement the kyoshi is opened. The shikko movement must be smooth and natural. During the movement one does not wobble forward, sideways or backwards. Steps should be of equal length.

Uke takes only one step at the opening and at the end, and tori takes two in all cases.

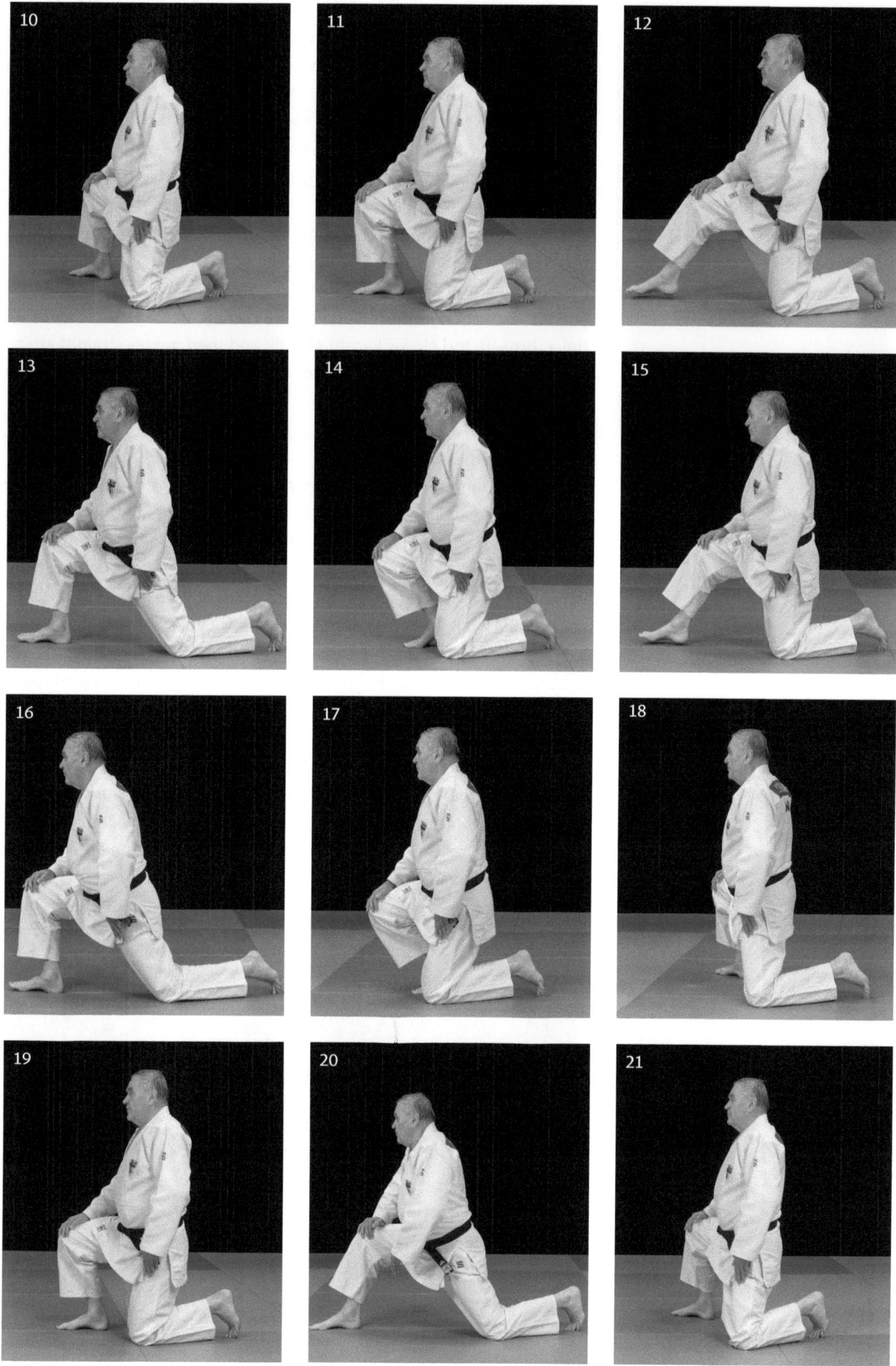

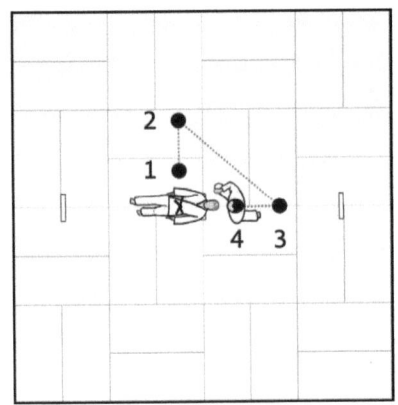

With the exception of the beginning and end of the technical groups tori shall always act in the same way when switching from the side of uke's head to uke's side or vice versa: Tori retreats from the chikama with two shikkos to the toma (points 1-2), opens kyoshi, stands up, moves with ayumi-ashi to another toma (points 2-3), descends, opens kyoshi, moves with two shikkos to the chikama (points 3-4) and opens kyoshi. At the beginning of the technique group tori starts from toma and at the end tori retreats to the toma.

Before performing each technique, tori takes an approach step from the chikama towards uke. The approach in kuzure-kami-shiho-gatame, hiza-gatame and ashi-garami are different from the other techniques and are explained in more detail in the context of these techniques. In the approach, tori closes kyoshi slightly and then moves straight ahead, bringing his shin close to uke. After this tori moves his left knee almost in contact with uke.

FOCUSING THE GAZE

At the start, during judogi adjustments, the last two techniques and the end, tori and uke are face to face. In these the eyes meet but there is no need to make eye contact. Side glances should be avoided.

When in the chikama kyoshi position tori's gaze is straight forward. While the gaze is directed forward tori must still be aware of the presence of uke at all times and must indicate this by his appearance. During the approaching step tori bends down and turns his face towards uke (22). At the end of the technique tori keeps his gaze on uke, retreats backwards to the chikama, straightens up, raises his gaze straight ahead and opens kyoshi.

Uke keeps his gaze in the distance at all times and does not look at what tori is doing. The exception to this are those arm locks in which uke looks at tori before attacking. When lying on his back uke should find some anchor point so that he knows at which position and in which direction he should be when tori moves him back into the correct place.

22

THE ROLE OF UKE

For the rhythm and realism of katame-no-kata uke's role is particularly important. Uke starts to act and tori's role is to react to this.

At the end of each technique, uke surrenders by tapping either with his hand or foot twice. The surrender is usually made with the hand and for the chokes made from the rear with the foot.

In ten techniques uke is lying on his back with the sole of the left foot on the mat and the knee slightly hooked. Both hands are relaxed with the fingers extended against the body and the head resting on the mat. The gaze is straight upwards (23). The neck and shoulders are on the centre line and uke's body is on the kata axis.

GOING SUPINE AND STANDING UP

Uke goes from kyoshi to supine three times during the kata: the first time at the beginning of the kata and twice after the adjustment of judogis. When going to the mat, uke places his right palm in front of him on the tatami with his fingers pointing to the left (24). The position of the palm is determined by where uke can naturally reach the right position on his back. Uke's right foot is still in kyoshi.

Uke supports himself on his right hand and left foot (25). He then lifts his left knee, threads his right leg under his body next to his left leg and sits down (26, 27). He moves his right hand with the fingers extended to his thigh and descends backwards to the ground (28). Tori is still in kyoshi.

On standing up from the supine position (28) uke rises to a sitting position and places his right hand behind his right buttock on the mat (29).

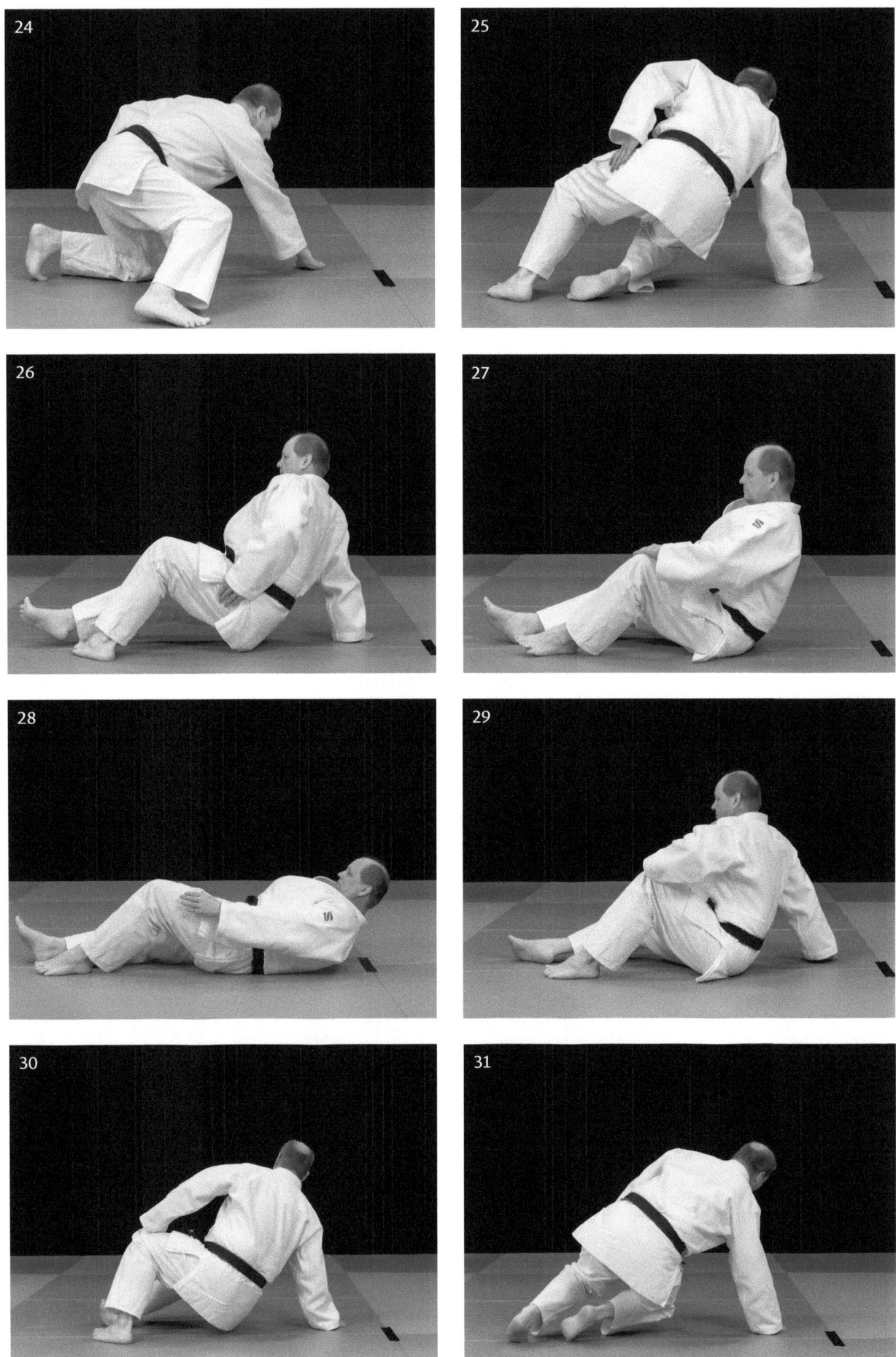

He supports his body with his left ball of the feet and right hand, raises his hips, turns his body to the right, changes the position of his right foot and stands up straight into kyoshi (30-33).

In the early Kodokan instructions for katame-no-kata the starting distance between tori and uke was about 3.6 m. In the 1960s, this was extended to about 5.5 m. Since then, the IJF has changed the distance even further to six metres. The number of steps has still remained the same in the Kodokan textbook. Thus it is difficult for a small uke to get to the right spot on his back. In different books, the number of shikkos after the opening step varies from zero to two.

SITTING POSITION

For chokes made from the rear uke is in the sitting position. He rises to a sitting position by sliding his hands from the sides of his thighs to his knees during the ascent without taking support from the mat. Uke bends both knees slightly. The left leg is more bent and the sole of the foot is at the shin of the right foot. The hands are relaxed on the knees and the fingers are extended, together and turned inwards (34).

Going back to the supine position is done in reverse order.

ADJUSTING THE JUDOGI

Tori and uke ensure that the judogi is neatly worn throughout the kata. Tori can adjust the judogi unnoticed when moving from one position to another. Uke can do the same during tori's transition. However, continuous adjustment and very visible, quick movements should be avoided. If the judogi becomes disarranged it must be adjusted at the appropriate time.

The actual adjustment of the judogi is done at the end of each technique group. It is done in kyoshi and face to face (35). Tori and uke should time their movements so that kyoshi is opened at the same time.

The adjustment can be done with simultaneous movements. First with both hands straighten the front tail corners of the jacket with one pull (36), then with one pull the rear tail corners (37) and finally a light straightening and tightening of the belt, if it is necessary (38). The belt must not be loosened and re-tied during the kata. However, if the belt has come totally loose, it is best to re-tie it calmly for example, during a judogi adjustment and continue the kata.

Osae-komi-waza

Osae-komi-waza contains the hold-down techniques of katame-no-kata. Practicing them provides tools for both tori and uke to develop their own understanding of what kind of solution is best suited to each situation. The Osae-komi-waza techniques are: KESA-GATAME (1), KATA-GATAME (2), KAMI-SHIHO-GATAME (3), YOKO-SHIHO-GATAME (4) and KUZURE-KAMI-SHIHO-GATAME (5).

Osae-komi-waza differs from nage-no-kata and other katame-no-kata wazas in that it presents important principles for both tori and uke. In the hold-down techniques three escapes and their counter movements are presented. Each of these contains slightly different details. After three attempts uke realizes he cannot escape and surrenders. This book describes one or two most common versions for each technique used in kata competitions. These given examples should not, however, limit the study of other options. Other alternatives may be presented, for example, in the grading examinations.

A good osae-komi-waza contains various technical elements that are expected to be included in the presentation and their absence can be considered a fault. Tori's and uke's movements must be seamlessly integrated with each other and have the right rhythm. Tori must respond promptly to uke's escape attempts, neither too early nor too late, creating a continuous cycle of action and reaction. After the reaction, a new situation arises, which uke tries to use immediately, and tori reacts again. Uke has a kind of a ready-made idea of how to build all three escapes. If tori were late on any of them, uke could escape. Rhythm is more important than speed, as rushing can ruin the kata. The challenge in osae-komi-waza is presenting each step clearly while maintaining efficiency.

Tori keeps the same hold throughout all uke's escape attempts. Feet move and one arm may even momentarily release, but the grip of both hands is never lost. In many techniques uke's right hand is lifted to the side at the beginning. This is done in a way that shows that at least one of the hands must always be in contact to uke.

Tori should avoid using excessive force in hold-down techniques, as it slows movements and hinders uke's performance. Tori must not attempt to control uke by hand force alone, but he must react to uke's

attempts to escape by changing his position or grip appropriately, while keeping a low centre of gravity to eliminate gaps. (7-9). The basis of the hold-down is the strong position of tori's feet (7, 9) and they are often in contact with uke's sides. Power is generated from the mat through the ball of the foot (7) or leg, aiding quick position changes and leg movements. Tori must not jump from one position to another in order not to lose control.

Uke's attempts to escape must be strong and such that, if tori would not counter the attempt each of them is so powerful that uke could escape (7-9). Uke must be able to use his body and all his limbs effectively. The feet are particularly important (7, 8). They transmit the power from the tatami to uke's movements. The legs allow uke to turn on his side, to move into a better line with tori, to push to roll tori over him, and to apply power to push the knee between tori and uke. Correct use of the legs also allows uke to use kinetic energy to enhance body rotations. Simply squeezing with the hands and body rotation alone are rarely sufficient for an effective escape.

ON THE PRACTICE OF HOLD-DOWN TECHNIQUES

The whole kata or one waza as a continuous performance should be practiced enough to avoid forgetting the sequence under pressure. Similarly, kneeling movements and taking the hold-down grips can be practised to gain confidence. Otherwise one should concentrate on practicing the techniques. This is the ultimate purpose of kata.

Repeated drills of escape attempts and counters will improve technical execution, timing and rhythm. Both tori and uke should have clearly visible the use of the whole body and the logic of what is being done. Every now and then it is worth practising so that uke makes a real attempt and gets away first. Then you start again and uke does the same escape attempt with the same power, which is countered by tori. Uke continues to the next stage, from which he escapes. This is continued until the entire sequence is completed. This gives a sense of realism to what is being done and gives both a sense of what the partner is doing.

When practising, the pair must be particularly careful that they do not start anticipating the movements of the other, thus helping the other in what he is doing. These include, for example, turning yourself before the other turns him, reacting before there is a need to react, and so on. This mistake must be avoided in all kata training.

Hold-down techniques can also be practised in tandoku-renshu by doing both the roles of tori (10-17) and uke (18-23). For example, for tori, the kesa-gatame hold-down position (10), first countering (11), second countering (12) and third countering (13), and the kata-gatame hold-down position (11), first countering (15), second countering (16) and third countering (17). For uke respectively, the first position of the kesa-ga-tame escape (19, 20), second escape (21) and third escape (22, 23). These are also well suited as initial warm-up movements.

KESA-GATAME   In English, kesa-gatame has been called "scarf hold". The name kesa (袈裟) does not refer to a common scarf, but to a robe worn by Buddhist monks which runs over the left shoulder to the right hip. In a similar manner in the kesa-gatame tori controls uke by pressing with his right side across the uke's chest. It should be noted that in the Kodokan catalogue of techniques kesa-gatame is a hold-down also known as hon-kesa-gatame. The technique in katame-no-kata is officially called kuzure-kesa-gatame. Perhaps this form has been chosen for the kata because it makes it easier to show different variations of hold-downs and escapes.

PRINCIPLE

The kata sets out the principles by which tori controls uke's right arm and shoulder as uke tries to escape. Tori uses different body and leg positions and takes support as needed from the tatami with his right hand.

Uke's principle is to break tori's strong hold-down, to get a gap between uke and tori and move into a position from which an escape attempt is possible.

TEACHING

Uke's escape attempts teach tori to understand the weak points of kuzure-kesa-gatame. He learns to maintain the basic control and his centre of gravity low as he changes the position of his feet. This hold-down technique teaches to understand the importance of sufficiently far away fulcrums. Tori also learns how to prevent uke from pushing the knee between tori and uke by spreading his legs.

Kuzure-kesa-gatame teaches uke three different types of escapes: the use of an arm lock for the escape, pushing the knee into the gap between uke and tori to break the hold-down and rolling tori over uke. At the same time it also teaches the use of the legs and the body in escape attempts.

IMPORTANT

At no time should tori release his grip on uke's right hand. Otherwise he will lose the control of uke's right shoulder.

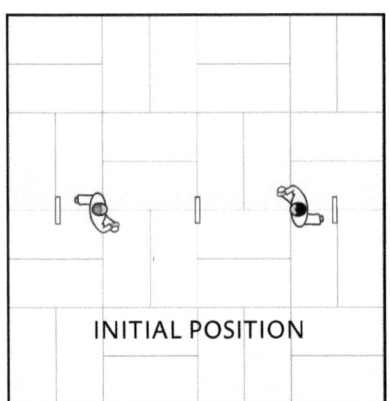

INITIAL POSITION

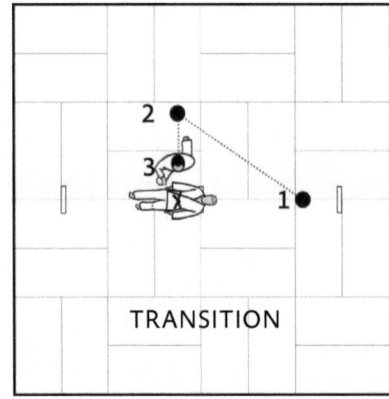

TRANSITION

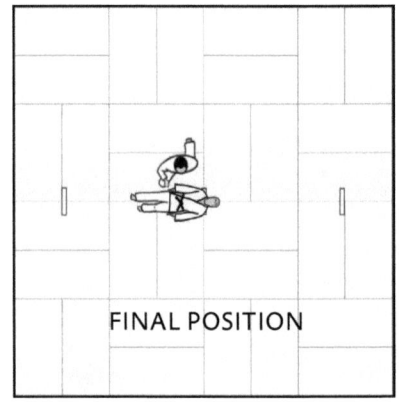

FINAL POSITION

START

After the opening step tori and uke descend to the kneeling position and open kyoshi. From this kyoshi begins the kesa-gatame technique and its evaluation in grading examination and in competition.

Uke takes one shikko step forward (1) and opens kyoshi. He then goes down on his back with his head towards tori (p. 174).

When uke has gone to supine position, tori moves to uke's side (2).

TAKING THE HOLD-DOWN

Tori stands up, walks to uke's right side, turns towards uke and stops standing in shizentai (3). He descends down, opens kyoshi (4), advances with two shikkos to the chikama and opens kyoshi (5). Tori takes an approach step forward from the chikama while turning his eyes to uke (6).

Tori takes with both hands a grip from uke's right arm so that the fingers of the left hand are under uke's upper arm and the fingers of the right hand are on the inside and under uke's forearm (7, 8).

Tori lifts uke's right arm with both hands to his own left armpit, encircles his left hand under and around uke's arm and takes grip of uke's sleeve close to his armpit. Tori squeezes with his upper arm uke's arm against his side (9, 10).

Tori then lowers his right knee to the tatami close to uke's right armpit, turns his body slightly to the left and brings his right hand under uke's left armpit to his shoulder (11). Tori lowers his right hip to the tatami and into contact with uke and moves his right foot forward. Tori places the right side of his chest firmly against uke's right breast and moves his left leg backwards to form a supporting triangle of legs and right arm (12). The left knee is on the mat. Tori's face is towards uke's face, and tori presses his head down slightly. When the hold-down is complete, tori gives the starting signal with a small but visible tightening of the grip.

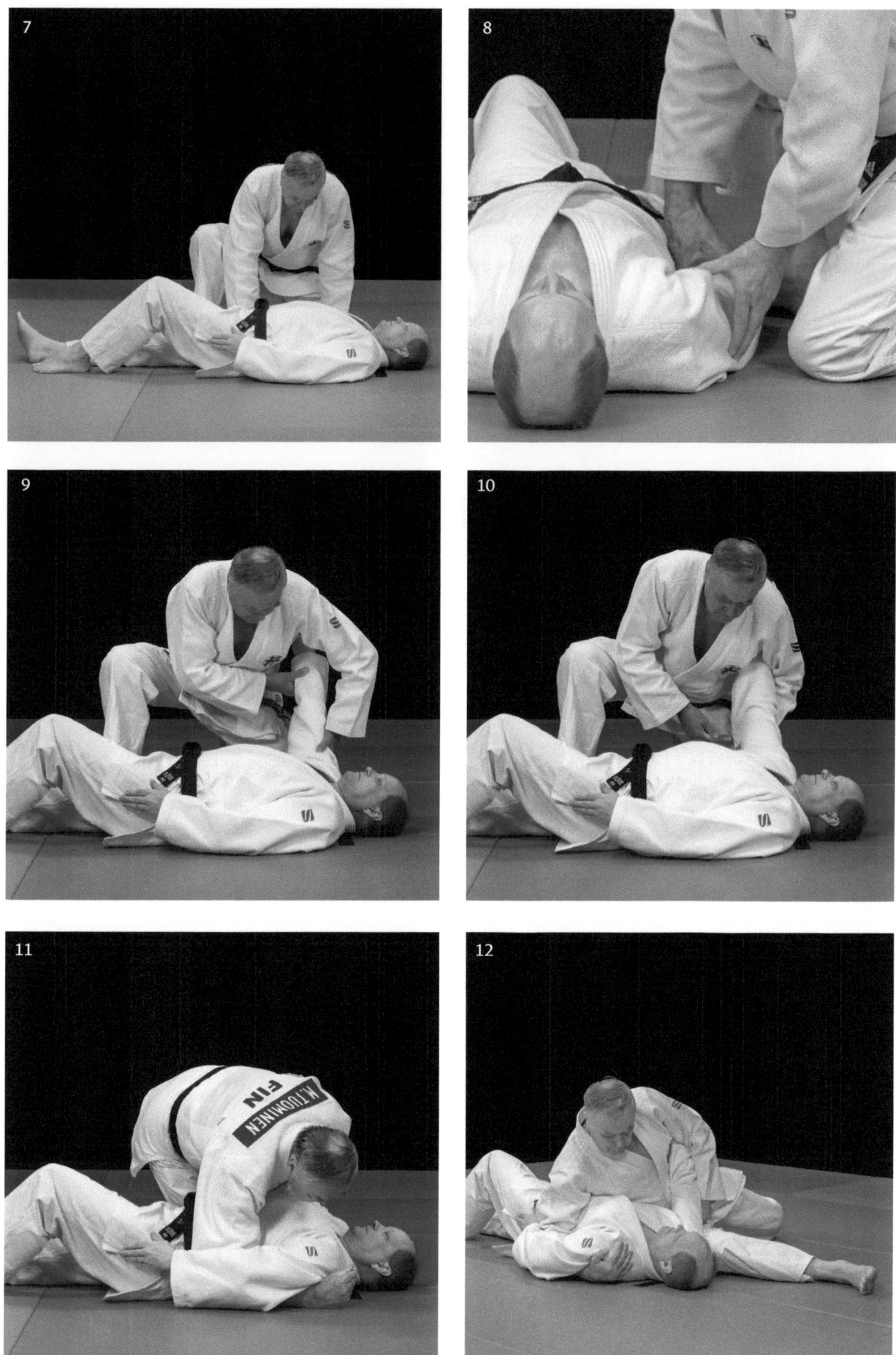

First escape:

Roll over using an arm lock

First, uke creates space for himself. He brings his left foot close to his buttocks and pushes off with his right foot to turn to his right side (13). Turning loosens tori's grip on uke's wrist and uke moves his right palm on tori's elbow joint. At the same time uke reaches his left palm on his right hand and he pulls tori's arm into a lock (14). The arm is now locked into a position from which uke can roll tori over his body.

Once in the grip, uke places the sole of his right foot on tatami and immediately starts to roll with a twist to the left (15). The force for the rotation comes from his right foot. The rotation can be strengthened with a swing with the left foot to the direction of the movement. Uke's aim is, for example, to end up into a hold-down. Tori stops the roll over by bringing his left leg over uke's longitudinal axis onto the mat (15). At the same time his position in relation to uke changes and the effect of the lock disappears. Tori can also extend his right hand to uke's left side as a support point, and to bring his right leg into contact with uke's right side (16). Tori tries to keep his hips as low as possible. The situation is worse for tori than the initial situation, because his pelvis is now off the mat.

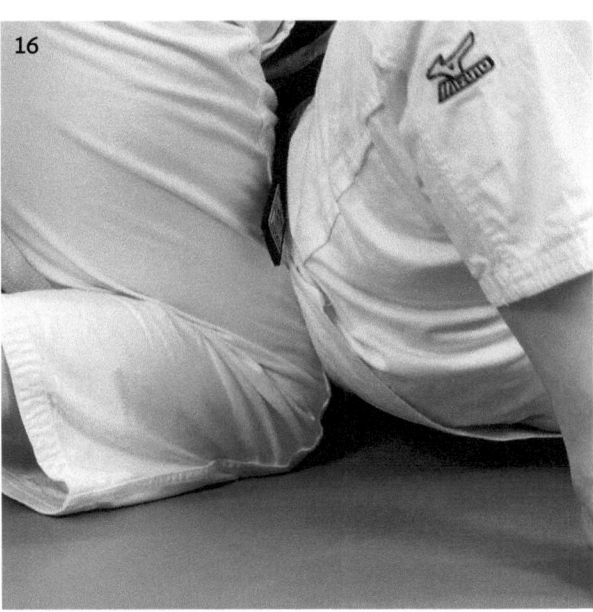

Second escape:

Knee in between tori and uke

Uke pushes off with his left foot and turns quickly to his right side to create space between tori and uke. If it's possible uke can grab with his left hand tori's belt at this stage. The right hand is still on tori's elbow. Pushing off with his left foot and steering with both hands, uke tries to push his right knee under tori's stomach (17).

When uke's knee is partially under tori, uke brings his left foot on top of tori. Uke's aim is to either capture tori's right leg or to get tori between his legs. Uke changes his grip to tori's belt at the latest at this point. Tori spreads his legs back into the kesa-ga-tame position and closes off the space for uke to bring his knee in between (18, 19). At the same time, tori's centre of gravity is moving forward.

Third escape:
ROLL OVER

Uke tries to take advantage of tori's forward movement. She keeps the position of her hands the same, if necessary she moves her body in better alignment with tori and seeks a strong position for her feet. Then uke squeezes tori against herself, rises on her shoulders, twists her body to the left and starts to roll tori over her (20, 21).

Tori stops the roll by bringing her left leg forward over uke's longitudinal axis onto the tatami (21). During the movement tori must keep her centre of gravity as low as possible. The speed to tori's movement comes from pushing her left foot and from uke's turning movement.

When uke realises that she cannot escape she surrenders by tapping twice with her left hand on tori's body.

In hold-down techniques the pair usually moves quite far from the initial position. Tori returns uke back to her place holding the hold-down grip. She makes the move and uke helps her during the transition as much as possible but with relatively small movements. Tori should ensure that uke is straight and her shoulder line is aligned correctly. Then tori holds the light hold-down grip for a short moment then rises to her knees and from there to the kneeling position. Tori does the same at the end of each hold-down technique.

After the transition tori takes the same grip as at the beginning of uke's right arm and returns the arm with both hands to uke's right side. As a general principle, tori returns the arm which she has moved.

Finally, tori retreats to the chikama and opens kyoshi. From this kyoshi the next technique begins.

! In Kesa-gatame the use of tori's legs and hips to change the position is emphasised. Tori must keep his centre of gravity low at all times and support points away from each other. Whenever possible, tori should keep either his side, hip or knee in contact with uke. With a left hand pull he can limit uke to use his right shoulder to turn to the right and to rise to a shoulder bridge. Tori's right hand on uke's left shoulder prevents uke from retreating further away and limits uke from lifting his shoulder up.

Uke should try to break tori's balanced position and get a small gap between uke and tori. When tori is forced to move, spaces are created, which uke utilizes to free himself.

It is very important for uke to know how to use his legs to move his body to be in line with tori. Uke's legs can be either in the same direction or in a different direction from tori's legs. The most force is needed for the escape if tori is directly on uke's side. In the first escape, uke moves his hips further away from tori and tries to pull tori over himself with the arm lock. In the third escape, he moves his legs closer to tori. This roll is best done in such a way that uke first rises to a shoulder bridge and pushes upwards with his hands towards his own right shoulder. As a result of this movement, tori's weight moves forward. Uke changes the direction of the movement to a strong twist to the left. The power for the turn comes from the legs and the midbody.

At the first and third escape, uke can obtain more power to the roll by swinging his left leg in the direction of the movement and twisting himself around his own longitudinal axis. There is very little variation in kesa-gatame escapes.

✱ Uke's first escape is shown as it succeeds (22). The options for the second escape is to either bring the knee completely to the other side of tori (23) or wrap tori's right leg with uke's legs (24). In the third escape uke uses a full body rotation (25). Tori's and uke's movements can be done either with the partner or alone as a tandoku-renshu in initial warm-up. These can also be done changing the roles. A great warm-up exercise is to block the first two escapes and let the third roll succeed, allowing uke to end up in kesa-gatame. Then, switch roles and continue to the third escape again.

KATA-GATAME   The "kata" in the name of kata-gatame refers to the fact that in this hold-down uke's shoulder is controlled. Since the kata-gatame involves both pressure on the neck and a strangulation element, its practice should be done cautiously and avoid excessive use of force and too fast movements.

PRINCIPLE

Tori's principle against uke's attempts to escape is to control uke's head and the right shoulder by positioning himself in a position from which it is difficult for uke to continue escape attempts.

Uke's principle is to try to loosen the head control and to get tori's legs moving. In doing so, he weakens tori's hold-down and creates space for the escape.

TEACHING

Kata-gatame teaches tori to understand the weaknesses of this hold-down technique and to block the most typical escape attempts. It teaches tori to change the position of the body and legs while maintaining the basic stance. It also teaches tori how to position himself, stay close to uke and keep his own position using the weight of his own body to push uke back.

Kata-gatame teaches uke three different principles of escape: using the strength of the arms and body to loosen the pressure on his head and neck, pushing his knee between tori and uke, and a somersault backwards.

IMPORTANT

Tori must maintain control of uke's shoulder and keep his hands together at all times.

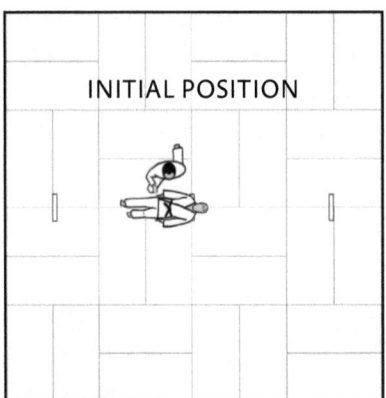

INITIAL POSITION

FINAL POSITION

Taking the hold-down

Tori takes an approach step from the chikama (1) towards uke (2). Then he grabs uke's right arm with both hands so that the fingers of the left hand are on the inside of uke's upper arm and the right hand fingers are on the outside of uke's wrist (3).

Tori lifts up uke's arm and then pushes it diagonally on uke's head (4). Kata-gatame is the only technique where tori grabs uke's arm like this while lifting it. In all other techniques, in which the arm is moved to the side, it is moved in the same way as in kesa-gatame.

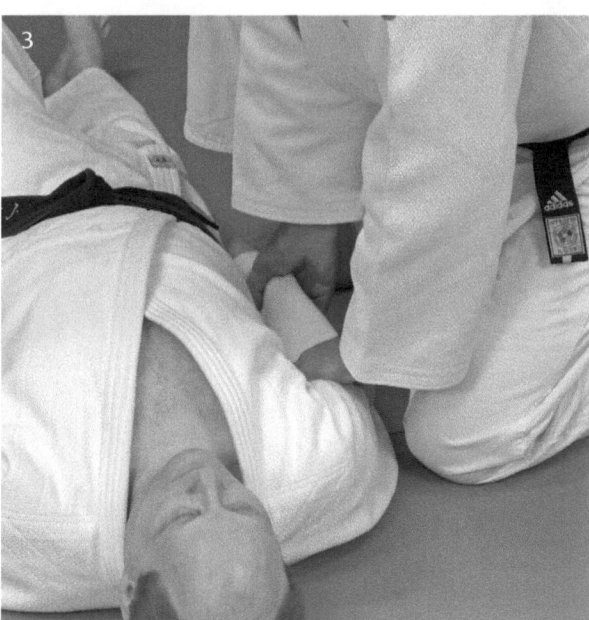

Tori turns his body to the left and presses with both hands uke's arm against his face. The arm is on uke's eyes. Then tori brings his right knee into contact with uke's right side, keeping the ball of the foot on tatami (5). The knee is slightly above uke's belt (8). Position of the knee on uke's side depends on the size difference between the pair.

Tori presses with his left hand uke's arm on uke's face and encircles his right hand around uke's neck (6). At the same time, tori outstretches his left leg straight to the left or slightly above uke's shoulder line (9). The position of the right foot is determined by where the triangle of legs is the most stable.

Tori puts his neck against uke's upper arm and attaches his palms together (7). The right hand is on the top. He ensures the control of uke's upper arm by pressing his head down close to the tatami and uke's head. Tori's body is at an angle of about 30 degrees to uke's body.

Tori closes the gap between the heads as small as possible, leans forward and tightens the hold-down (9). Tori's right arm, head and left shoulder form clamps between which uke's head and right upper arm are held. Tori's head is off the mat. The purpose of the hold-down technique is not to squeeze uke's neck tightly with the hands, but for tori to lean slightly forward with the force of the legs, so that

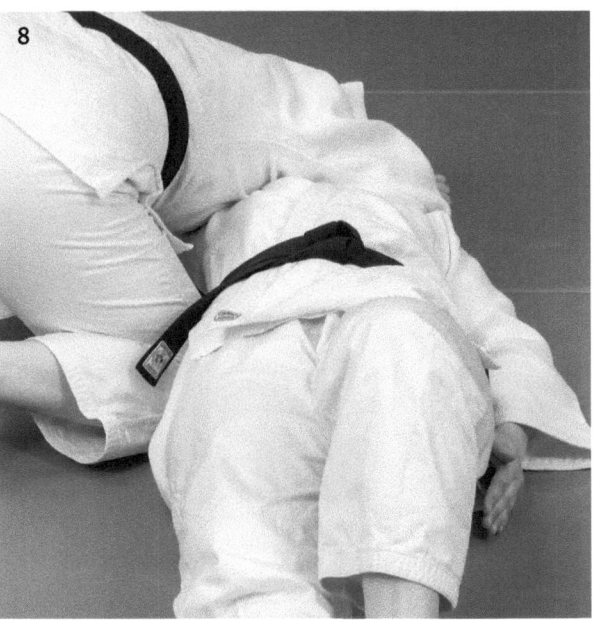

the force from tori's shoulder is directed diagonally through uke's right upper arm towards the mat. At the same time, uke's chin rises slightly upwards, making it more difficult for him to escape.

FIRST ESCAPE:
RELEASE OF UKE'S RIGHT ARM

Uke closes his right hand into a fist, puts the palm of his left hand onto the fist of his right hand and brings the soles of his feet to the tatami (10, 11). Uke pushes off with his feet, turns to his right side and using the strength of his body pushes his elbow towards tori's head. The arms are in line, and the body is slightly bridged. Uke tries to create space to slip his arm to the other side of tori's head. His aim is to free himself by, for example, flipping tori on his back. Tori counters by pressing his head against the tatami, by getting down on his knees and following uke's movements with his body (12). It is also possible for tori to keep kata-gatame position and right knee in contact with uke. The most important thing is that tori controls uke with his body movements and his head and not just by squeezing uke with his arms. Uke makes an attempt with his elbow twice or three times.

When finishing the attempts, uke is slightly on his right side facing tori. He now has the opportunity to take advantage of the empty space under tori.

Second escape:
Knee between tori and uke

Uke turns more to his right side and reaches out with his left hand to take a grip of tori's belt (13). At the same time, he pushes off with his left foot, moves his hips further away from tori and releases his right side from tori's knee control. Pushing off with his left foot and pulling with his left hand, uke tries to push his right knee under tori's stomach (14). The knee must be lifted off the mat, as tori's right knee prevents uke from moving his leg along the mat. In addition, uke can bring his left foot on tori's back. Uke's aim is to get his legs around tori. Another escape option is pushing with the legs tori further away and doing, for example, an arm lock.

Tori moves his left leg forward (foot sole on the mat) and spreads his right leg widely into a kesa-gatame position while maintaining the control of uke's upper arm with his head and handhold (15, 16).

After spreading his legs wide tori's control of uke is no longer as strong as in the original hold-down.

THIRD ESCAPE:
BACKWARD SOMERSAULT

Uke tries to take advantage of the fact that tori's weight is now in the front. Uke moves his lower body far to the left (17) and disengages from tori's body contact. While the movement is still in progress, uke pushes off with his right foot and attempts a backward somersault over his left shoulder and head. The somersault can be boosted by taking support with the left elbow on the mat (18).

Tori counters the attempt by going down on his stomach next to uke's body, straightening his right leg and pushing uke back to the mat (19, 20). When pushing uke back, tori keeps his hips very low. Another method often used is that tori goes on all fours (21). The third way is to return back to the kata-gatame position (22).

After realising that he cannot escape, uke surrenders with tapping twice on tori's body.

Tori and uke return to their original position. Tori holds the light original hold-down for a short time, rises on his knees and from there continues to kneeling position, takes the same grip of uke's arm as in the beginning and returns the arm to uke's right side. Tori retreats to the chikama and opens kyoshi.

! Tori should try to keep the hips low and the supporting points far apart. By shifting his centre of gravity, tori ensures that his weight is at the longest possible distance away from uke.

Uke must be able to use his feet to change the position of his body in relation to tori. This is particularly important in the last escape, where a change in the angle between tori and uke will greatly improve the chances to escape.

There is a lot of variation in tori's first and third counter movements of kata-gatame.

In the first escape, uke can push off with his feet and push tori onto his back after he has freed his right arm (23, 24). Uke's second option is to roll tori over. In the second escape, uke can wrap the legs around tori's leg (25) or do an arm lock (26). When the somersault succeeds, uke has a good control of tori's right arm and he can twist tori over him (27, 28). The roles of tori and uke can be practised either with a partner or as a tando-ku-renshu in the initial warm-up. A good warm-up is that uke counters all three escapes and then wraps the right arm around tori's neck, rolls tori over to the left, ends up in kata-gatame, and continues in tori's role.

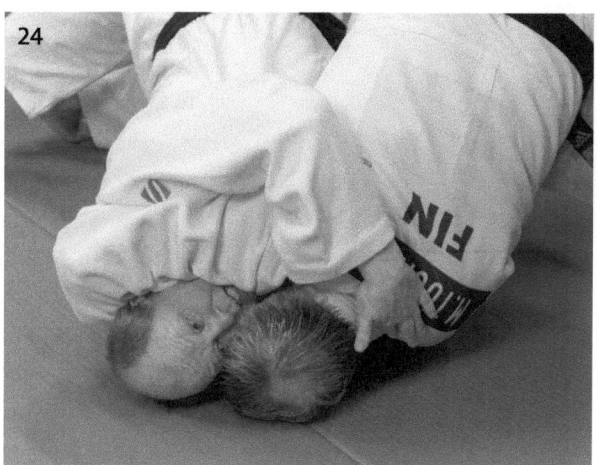

KAMI-SHIHO-GATAME The name of the shiho-gatame hold-downs refers to the four directions. The basic shape of the hold-down technique is formed by tori's arms and legs, creating a four-point structure.

PRINCIPLE

In kami-shiho-gatame, tori's principle is to control uke's upper body against his escape attempts in various situations. Tori does this by using his body weight and by limiting the movements of uke's hips with his hands and by keeping the support points of his own legs as wide as possible.

Uke's principle is to break the lateral support of tori's legs and get himself into a position to be able to rotate around his own longitudinal axis. The second principle is to increase distance and release his upper body from tori's control.

TEACHING

Kami-shiho-gatame is the weakest against lateral movement. Katame-no-kata teaches tori to counter uke's most typical escape attempts. Against uke's lateral thrusts tori learns to bring support points to the side. If uke tries to turn onto his stomach tori uses his body weight, positioning and legs.

Kami-shiho-gatame teaches uke three different escapes: the first is based on tori's counter-reaction and the other two are based on increasing the distance from tori. Uke learns that tightly joined bodies easily rotate around a longitudinal axis. Tori has a relatively small lever force to prevent rapid sideways spins.

IMPORTANT

Because the rotations on tori's longitudinal axis are fast, tori must be able to quickly bring the support points to the side.

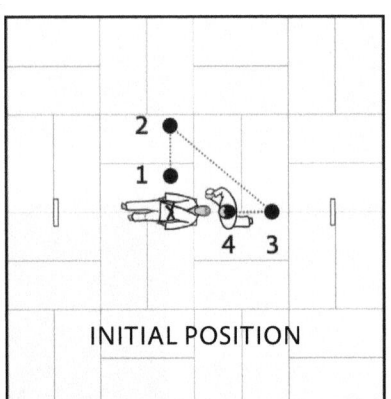

INITIAL POSITION

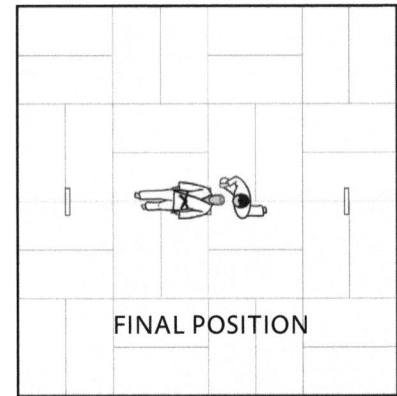

FINAL POSITION

TAKING THE HOLD-DOWN

Tori retreats to the toma, opens kyoshi, stands up, moves to the side of uke's head (1), descends and opens kyoshi (2). He then moves with two shikko steps into chikama and opens kyoshi (3).

Tori takes an approach step from the chikama towards uke bringing his left knee close to uke's ear and puts his right knee to the mat on the other side of uke's head (4). The balls of the feet are still on the mat. Then he slides his both palms along the mat under uke's shoulders (5), grabs uke's belt from the side with a normal grip and controls with both arms uke's shoulders (6). The thumbs are inside the belt and elbows are close to uke. At this point, uke should turn his face to the left. Finally, tori presses his chest against uke's chest and turns his face to the left. Tori should not move too far over uke's chest, so that the position remains stable.

After getting the hand grip, tori moves first one and then the other knee closer to uke's shoulders. He straightens his insteps on the mat, lowers his hips and tightens the hold-down (7). Tori must have a sturdy position with his insteps on the mat and centre of gravity low. Tori's head and chest control uke's chest and shoulders and his hands control uke's hips. The force is directed diagonally downwards and holds uke's shoulders in the mat.

FIRST ESCAPE:
ROLL TO THE LEFT
Uke puts the left hand on tori's neck and right hand onto tori's back (8). The hands can also be the other way round. Uke puts the sole of the left foot on the tatami and makes a twisting movement to the right, pushing tori mainly with the left hand (9). Uke's hand grip is still quite loose. Tori resists the movement, puts the balls of the feet onto tatami and pushes with the body slightly against. Uke takes advantage of tori's reaction, squeezes tori against with both hands, pushes off with the right foot, and with a powerful twist of the body to the left starts to roll tori over the body (10).

It is not specified in which direction uke is trying to roll tori over. However, in kata competitions, the turn is to the left, with the left hand being uke's lower hand (10).

Tori counters uke's rolling by bringing the left leg straight out to the side against the rotation (10). Tori's right knee is still on the mat.

Uke continues to twist to the left but loosens her pull towards herself. As uke is now on her left side, tori is not able to apply as much pressure to uke's chest.

SECOND ESCAPE:
TURNING RIGHT ONTO HER STOMACH
Uke quickly turns back onto the back, while trying to maintain the space that is now between tori and uke. Uke pushes the left hand under tori's chin (11), pushing off with the left foot, swings the hips

to the right and tries to get free by twisting onto the stomach (12, 13). Tori counters the attempt by quickly bringing the left knee back to the mat and by moving against uke's twist to uke's right side. Tori keeps the hips low and pushes with the upper body uke back onto her back (13, 14). The other option for tori is to straighten the right foot to the side.

Uke uses the left forearm to push tori by the neck and retreats further away from underneath tori. Tori no longer has a good control of uke's upper body, and uke has both of her hands free.

Third escape:
Somersault onto tori's back

Uke places her hands on tori's shoulders. She pushes with her hands while pulling herself with her legs away from tori (15, 16). Tori tries to correct her own position and follows uke (16).

When uke gets further away, she grabs tori's shoulders with her hands. Another possibility is to put the hands with fingers straight into tori's armpits to take support from tori's body. However, changing the grip can give tori time to come back into contact with uke, and it may be interpreted as an unnecessary movement. Uke bends her body backwards in a somersault (17). From this point on uke has two possible ways to continue: either try to push the legs into tori's groin or try to put the knees against tori's shoulders. The latter requires a greater distance between tori and uke than the first one.

Tori will counter the attempt by lifting the knees off the mat, pushing with the head or shoulder and the chest from uke's stomach to force uke back to the mat, while tightening the grip of the hands (18, 19). Tori has the legs spread wide, and the force is directed diagonally downwards to the front. Tori's knees may also be bend.

When uke realises that he cannot escape, he surrenders by tapping twice on tori's body. Tori and uke return to their original position. Tori keeps the hold-down briefly, gets up on his knees and from there to a kneeling position.

Tori releases his grip, retreats to the chikama and opens kyoshi (20). Uke moves his own hands back.

! In kami-shiho-gatame, tori must try to keep his body in line with uke's body but be careful to avoid a situation where tori's longitudinal axis is in line with either side of uke. Tori must keep his centre of gravity low and avoid getting too deep down into uke's lap.

Tori shall not apply excessive squeezing in hold-down. In this way he will maintain his ability to react quickly to uke's movements. He must also be on his toes as soon as uke makes his first attempt, in order to be able to push off with his feet. Tori must be ready at all times to bring his foot to the side for support.

In kami-shiho-gatame, it is important to find a common rhythm for the escapes and counter actions. Uke's escape attempts must be followed by a clear counter, followed by the next attempt by uke. Also the last escape attempt and its counter-attack must be realistic.

There are differences in the kami-shiho-gatame counter actions. For example, for the first escape, tori may go down lying on his stomach on the opposite side of uke. In the second escape, tori may move against the rotation or move his leg to the side or to the back (21).

21

* In the first escape, uke keeps tori close to her and turns around (22, 23). In the second escape, uke must push her arm far enough under tori's throat and turn onto her stomach (24 , 25). The third escape requires a sufficient distance and agility (26, 27). The first escape in particular is a good practice move, where immediately after uke's roll the roles can be switched and the movement is continued alternately. As with kesa-gatame and kata-gatame, all blocks can be performed, returning back to the starting position, from which the first escape is executed and roles are switched again.

YOKO-SHIHO-GATAME

The name yoko-shiho-gatame refers to the fact that uke is controlled from the side by means of four support points. This hold-down allows uke a good opportunity to move, so tori must be ready to react to uke's movements quickly.

PRINCIPLE

Tori's principle against uke's attempts is to control with his chest and left hand uke's upper body and to control with the grip of his right hand uke's hips. Tori uses his knees as support points on the right side of uke's body.

Uke's principle is to use his movements to eliminate tori's supports and create space for the escape. By moving his body and turning on his side, uke increases the distance to tori and tries to make tori to move. As tori moves, his centre of gravity rises higher, which enables him to roll, for example.

TEACHING

Yoko-shiho-gatame teaches tori the weak directions of the hold-down technique and demonstrates different ways of countering the escape attempts. It teaches how to eliminate uke's attempts by changing the position of his feet and how to use the whole body, including the head, in counters. One well-held control point is enough, when the other limbs are supporting this one control.

Yoko-shiho-gatame teaches uke three different types of escapes when he is controlled from the side: the use of the leg to catch tori's head, the pushing of the knee between tori and uke, and a roll over. It further teaches the use of the body and legs in a situation where uke's left foot and right hand movements are limited.

IMPORTANT

Keeping control of uke's right side, the head and the pelvis.

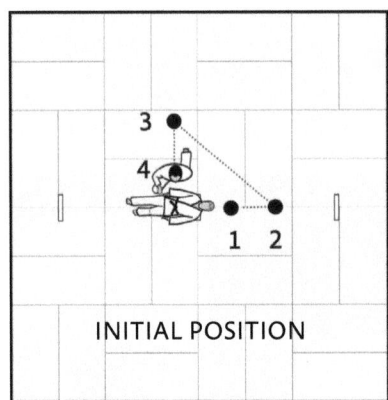

INITIAL POSITION

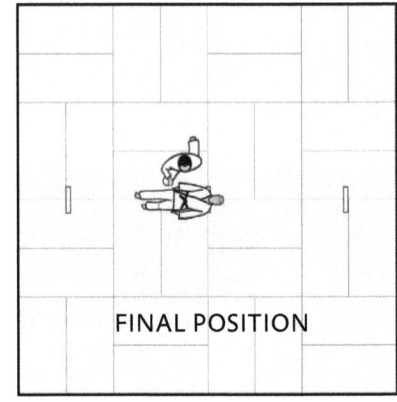

FINAL POSITION

Taking the hold-down

Tori retreats to the toma, opens kyoshi, stands up, walks to uke's right side to the toma, lowers himself down and opens kyoshi. He then moves with two shikkos to the chikama and opens kyoshi.

Tori takes an approach step from the chikama towards uke. Then he lifts uke's right arm with the same grip he used in the kesa-gatame onto his left side and moves his right hand with thumb upwards into uke's armpit (1). Tori releases this control only after he has gained control with his other hand. Tori brings his left knee to uke's armpit. He puts his left hand thumb next to the knot in uke's belt, slides his hand downwards and pushes the belt towards uke's legs to make it easier for him to take a grip with his right hand (2, 3). Then tori brings his right knee to the mat and in contact with uke's hips, runs his right arm between uke's legs and takes grip of uke's belt (4). The arm comes around uke's buttock, not the thigh. The thumb is inside the belt. Tori's toes are still against the tatami. Lastly, tori brings his left arm around uke's neck and takes a normal grip on uke's left upper lapel (5). The hand on the upper lapel does not need not be very far. It is enough when it is roughly close to uke's ear.

Tori pushes both knees into contact with uke's side, puts his insteps onto the tatami and turns his head to the left. Tori's head is slightly upwards from uke's belt and at the level of with uke's left side. Tori tightens the hold-down by pulling uke with both hands towards his own belt and pressing uke against the tatami with his body (5).

FIRST ESCAPE:
CONTROL OF TORI'S HEAD WITH THE FEET
Uke places the left hand on tori's neck and right hand on tori's right side (6, 7). Uke pushes off with his right foot in the direction of his head and pushes tori with both hands, causing tori to move towards uke's feet. At the same time, uke raises his left leg and tries to capture uke's head behind his knee (8). Uke's aim is to get tori's head between the legs and make a sankaku-jime, ude-gatame or continue with some other technique. Uke does the attempt two or three times.

Tori counters the attempt by pushing his neck against uke's bent left leg (8). Another option to counter is to pull back and press the head firmly against uke's body. Tori can also straighten his right leg behind. In this case, however, the knee control over uke is weakened and tori must be ready to bring his knee into contact with uke as soon as uke continues with other escape attempts.

Second escape:
Knee between tori and uke

Uke pushes with his left foot and turns on his right side further away from tori (9). At the same time, uke takes a grip with his left hand from tori's belt and pushes his right elbow under tori's stomach. If uke does not reach to take a grip of the belt, the grip must be taken as close to the belt as possible. Pushing off with his left foot and pulling with his hands, uke pushes his right knee under tori's stomach (10). Uke's aim is to wrap his legs around tori.

Tori counters the attempt by spreading his left leg towards uke's legs (11). As a result of the spreading of his feet wide the control over uke's upper body is weakened and the centre of gravity shifts towards the legs. The spreading of the legs can also be done towards uke's head.

THIRD ESCAPE:
ROLL OVER

Uke's upper body is now quite free. He pushes off with his left foot himself further away from tori. If Uke does not yet have a grip on tori's belt, he grabs it from the back and places his right elbow on tori's stomach (18). Tori tries to correct his position and improve his control over uke and returns back on his knees. Uke brings his right foot close to his own buttocks, pushes off with his right foot and starts a strong turn to the left to roll tori over him (12). Uke should try to use tori's approach movement for his benefit and bring tori slightly over uke's shoulders over him. Also a straight roll around the longitudinal axis is possible.

Tori will counter the attempt by straightening and spreading his legs, keeping his hips down and supporting his forehead to the mat on the left side of uke's body (13). The place of tori's head on the mat depends on the pair's size difference and on how far tori brings his left foot to the tatami. The second option for tori to counter is to shift his centre of gravity to the direction of uke's head and bring the left foot to the level of uke's head or pass it. This option is particularly useful when tori has countered by spreading his legs wide towards uke's head.

After realising that he cannot escape, uke will surrender by tapping twice to tori's body with his hand.

Tori and uke return to their original position. Tori keeps the hold-down for a short moment. Then he releases his right hand from uke's belt, takes a grip of uke's right arm with both of his hands, rises to a kneeling position and lifts uke's arm back to its place.

Tori retreats to the chikama and opens kyoshi.

! Tori must try to keep his centre of gravity low at all times, control uke's hands and chest, and to spread as wide as possible. Tori's right knee controls uke's hips and the left knee limits the movements of uke's right shoulder. Tori uses his upper body to push uke's chest and stomach downwards to the mat. Especially in the last escape, uke has a very strong position. Tori must be able to bring his head or left leg quickly to the mat and keep his hips low. With these movements he can eliminate uke's powerful elbow against his stomach.

The movements of the yoko-shiho-gatame are usually similar to each other except for the spreading of the legs in the second escape towards uke's head.

In the first escape uke may end, for example, in an arm lock (14, 15), to a strangle or to a rolling tori over uke. In the second escape, uke wraps tori's foot between the legs (16, 17). In the third escape, a strong hand-hold (18) and the legs are used to roll tori over. From yoko-shiho-gatame, a warm-up can also be performed by executing the first two escapes with blocks, allowing the third roll to succeed, resulting in uke ending up in yoko-shiho-gatame and continuing as tori.

A really good warm-up is to perform all four previous hold-down sequences in the following order as a continuous movement: yoko-shi-ho-gatame, kesa-gatame, kata-gatame, and kami-shiho-gatame.

KUZURE-KAMI-SHIHO-GATAME

Kuzure-kami-shiho-gatame is a four-point hold-down, where the best control is from uke's right shoulder. Tori's support points are diagonally across uke and therefore this hold-down is not as weak in longitudinal or lateral directions than kami-shiho-gatame. Uke's left arm and lower body remain relatively free, however.

PRINCIPLE

Tori's principle is to resist uke's attempts to escape by controlling uke's right shoulder. Tori tries to keep his centre of gravity low and the angle in relation to uke the same.

Uke's principle is to release his right arm first. Then he tries to increase the distance and break the strong position of tori's legs. As uke gets further away from tori and gets him moving, it is easier for uke to attempt an escape.

TEACHING

Kuzure-kami-shiho-gatame teaches tori to understand the weak points of this hold-down and to control uke by holding a grip from his collar and keeping his shoulders in contact with the mat. At the same time, it teaches tori how to counter uke's attempts to escape and make them ineffective with body movements.

Kuzure-kami-shiho-gatame teaches uke three principles to escape: the use of the space created by the thrust of both hands and turning himself on his stomach, use of the left hand and the knee to release the grip, and rolling over. In all of these, the correct use of his feet and the positioning of his body in relation to tori's are of great importance.

IMPORTANT

Control of uke's right shoulder and control of his upper body with the chest.

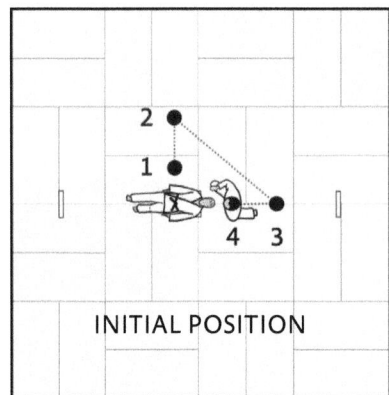

INITIAL POSITION

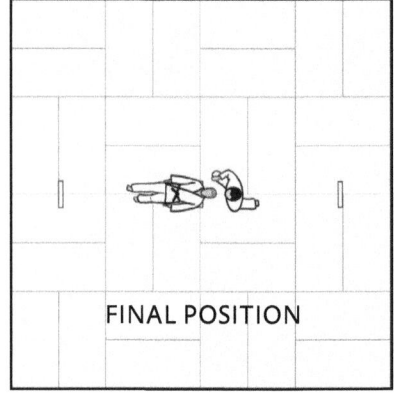

FINAL POSITION

TAKING THE HOLD-DOWN

As in kami-shiho-gatame, tori moves from uke's right side chikama to uke's head side to the chikama and opens kyoshi.

Tori takes an approach step from the chikama towards uke's head. As with the other approach steps, tori does not close the kyoshi, but the right foot moves almost directly forward. Tori then moves with another longer step diagonally to the right. At the same time he turns to the left towards uke at an angle of about 45 degrees (1).

With his right hand, tori grabs uke's right wrist from the inside, lifts the arm on his right thigh and holds it with both hands (2). Then he reaches out

with his right hand a grip of uke's collar under uke's right shoulder (3). The back of the hand is against the tatami and the fingers inside the collar (4). Tori descends his right knee, reaches out with his left hand a grip from uke's belt under his left shoulder (5). Tori puts his insteps against tatami and presses his hips down. Tori's left thumb is inside uke's belt and the arm controls uke's shoulder.

Tori controls uke by pressing his chest diagonally onto uke's right chest and tightens the hold-down by pulling uke's body towards him with both hands (6).

FIRST ESCAPE:
MAKING SPACE WITH THE RIGHT HAND
AND TURNING ONTO HIS STOMACH
Uke puts his left hand in a v-shape on tori's neck (7). Uke can in the beginning make some space by pushing off with his feet and moving his body more in line with tori. Pushing off with his left foot and pushing with his left hand, uke turns onto his right side and moves his right hand in a fist to tori's groin (8). Uke tries to turn over on his stomach by pushing with his hands and twisting his body vigorously to the right.

As soon as uke starts his escape attempt, tori puts his toes onto the tatami. Tori spreads simultaneously both of his feet and ends up in an ushiro-kesa-gatame hold-down to the right side of uke, eliminating thus the power of uke's right hand (9). Tori's control of uke's upper body, however, is impaired and the posture is weak.

SECOND ESCAPE:
LEFT KNEE BETWEEN TORI AND UKE
AND TURNING ON HIS STOMACH
Uke is lying slightly on his right side, and he turns his left forearm against tori's neck. Uke's fingers are pointing down. He can also hold his left hand against tori's neck (10). Uke grabs tori's belt with his right hand and pushes tori with his hands further away and upwards (11). The grip can also be taken earlier. Immediately after uke's push with the fist tori reacts to this and returns back on his knees (11).

Uke tries to push his left knee between tori and uke in an attempt to gain more strength and make more space to turn around on his stomach or on his knees (11). Tori counters the attempt by turning his body against the push and pressing with his body pushes uke back to the tatami (12). Due to uke's push, there is still space between tori and uke and tori must try to gain better control.

THIRD ESCAPE:
ROLL OVER
Uke pushes off with his left foot and reaches over with his left hand to take a grip of tori's belt. If uke cannot reach the belt, he grabs the judogi. Uke's right hand grip is on tori's belt (12). After getting the left hand grip, uke still pushes off towards tori, causing tori to push back. Uke uses the counter reaction and tries to roll tori over him by turning around his longitudinal axis (13).

Tori counters by quickly bringing his left foot against the roll over and keeping his hips low (14). Another option for tori is to straighten the right leg and lower his weight far back (15). After noticing that he cannot escape, uke surrenders by tapping twice on tori's body.

Tori moves uke to the original position. He keeps the hold-down for a brief moment, rises on his knees, then to the kneeling position and returns with both hands uke's right arm back in place. After this, tori returns with a small step back to the side of uke's head, then he takes one step to the chikama and opens kyoshi. Often tori will also move directly with one step to the chikama.

! Kuzure-kami-shiho-gatame is perhaps the most difficult of the kata hold-down techniques to execute naturally. The rhythm and the movements of tori and uke are very important. Tori who is applying too much force will prevent uke from doing sensible escape attempts and will ruin the performance.

When moving, tori must keep his toes on the mat and uke's right shoulder under control. Uke must not be controlled solely with arms but with the strength of the whole body. The pressure of the body must be applied diagonally forward and downward. If necessary, tori can roll uke back to his place by pressing with his upper body.

✱ At the first escape, uke turns onto her stomach (16, 17). At the second escape, uke uses his knee to push tori's grip looser, then he can turn onto his stomach or on his knees (18, 19). In the third escape, uke uses the legs and the turn of his whole body to roll tori over (20, 21).

After osaekomi-waza

ADJUSTING THE JUDOGI

Tori retreats two steps backwards to a distance of toma from uke. When tori retreats, uke rises to a sitting position with his hands on his thighs. Then uke places his right hand behind his right buttock on the tatami, supports his body on his left foot and right hand, lifts his hips, turns his body to the right, moves his right foot and stands up straight into a kyoshi (p. 174, 175). At the same time, tori stops in toma and opens kyoshi. When kyoshis are opened, tori and uke adjust their judogis.

The osae-komi-waza is completed.

If a short version of the katame-no-kata is performed, tori and uke continue directly with the closing ceremonies.

Shime-waza

Judo chokes are applied either to the blood vessels to the head or to the trachea. Vascular strangulations squeeze either the arteries, veins or both together. Their effectiveness is based on the use of pressure on the muscle involved in nodding, turning, and tilting the head (sternocleidomastoid). The carotid arteries and veins are protected by this muscle. The compression blocks the blood flow and, if prolonged, causes a loss of consciousness. Tracheal compressions cause pain and also partially obstruct the respiratory flow. Some strangles have all these elements.

Shime-waza techniques are KATA-JUJI-JIME (1), HADAKA-JIME (2), OKURI-ERI-JIME (3), KATAHA-JIME (4) and GYAKU-JUJI-JIME (5). First and the last belong to the juji-jime strangles. The name origins from the fact that the hands are crossed. Ju in Japanese is ten and its character (十) resembles a plus sign or cross. They and okuri-eri-jime and kataha-jime are vascular strangles. Hadaka-jime is a strangle effecting at the throat. It involves the sharp edge of the wrist or arm pressing on uke's trachea.

No strangle of any kind may be performed on anyone under the age of 15. The teaching of strangles to people below green belt must be done with caution and discretion. Similarly, in the case of elderly people or those with cardiovascular disease it is advisable to avoid hard strangles and to do them gently in the kata.

For all strangles, tori must first control uke before he can perform a successful strangle. For control, he uses the whole body and his limbs. Similarly, the entire body must be used for the movement leading to the choke. Strangulation with the hands alone rarely produces the desired result. In strangulation done on top of uke, the kata-juji-jime and gyaku-juji-jime, tori controls uke, especially with his legs (6). Poor leg control leads to a poor strangle.

In strangles from behind i.e. in hadaka-jime, okuri-eri-jime and kata-ha-jime, tori puts uke in a position where it is difficult for uke to defend (7). In addition, in the first two of these, the movements of uke's head are restricted by tori's head.

When performing kata, the most important thing is to show a technically correct performance, rather than the effectiveness of the strangle. Power is only important in kata competitions, and there, experienced competitors know each other's limits. A technically correctly executed choke requires little hand power and its effect can come as a surprise. For this reason, it is worth practising chokes individually and studying with the partner how they work.

The rhythm of the strangulation is important. The strangle grip is taken calmly, and the strangulation itself is done relatively quickly.

In all chokes, uke tries to defend himself (6, 7). Uke tries firstly to reduce the pressure on the strangling hands and secondly to escape the situation. The defence must be real, and it must be initiated only once the strangulation has started. Escapes should also be practised to the point of release, so that both tori and uke become aware of the importance of attack and defence. In all escapes, however, it is important to remember caution, as tori has a tight grip on uke's neck.

6

KATA-JUJI-JIME The English name for kata-juji-jime has often been 'half cross strangle.' However, this translation might not be entirely accurate, as the term 'kata' (片) in Japanese likely refers to the asymmetrical positioning of the hands rather than implying 'half' in the sense of incompleteness or partiality.

PRINCIPLE

Tori's principle is to take a grip on uke's lapels and use the full body strength and arm movement for an effective choke. Correct hand position is more important than strength. When done correctly the choke should be applied to the muscles of the neck and not to uke's trachea.

TEACHING

Tori learns through kata-juji-jime a technically correct execution of the strangulation and to use his legs for a strong control.

For uke, the choke teaches one possible way to escape. In the kata uke is not given the opportunity for a real escape, but in randori training he must try to prevent the choke at the earliest possible stage. In order to escape, uke must be able to loosen the choke and break tori's tight leg control.

IMPORTANT

Correct direction of arm movements and use of body weight in the choke.

INITIAL POSITION

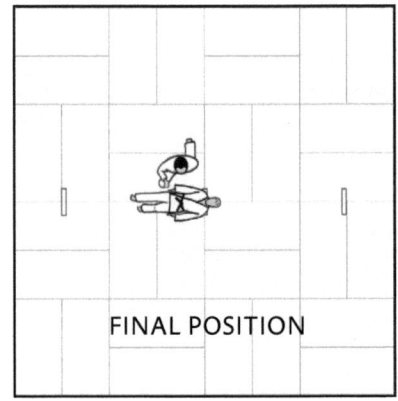

FINAL POSITION

EXECUTION

After adjustment of judogis, uke goes into a supine position in the same way and to the same place as at the beginning.

When uke is on his back, tori stands up and moves to uke's right side to the toma (1), descends to a kneeling position, opens kyoshi, then moves forward with two shikkos (2) to the chikama and again opens kyoshi.

Tori takes a short step forward to approach uke from the chikama, grabs uke's right arm with both hands in the same way as in kesa-gatame and moves uke's arm to his own left side (3).

Tori moves his right hand to uke's right armpit and presses with his thumb lightly uke's shoulder towards the tatami (4).

Tori then moves his left knee close to uke's armpit (5). While still pressing with the right thumb uke's right shoulder to the mat, tori slides his left hand as deep as possible into uke's left lapel (6) and takes a grip. Fingers are inside the lapel, palm is up and thumb is on the outside.

Tori pushes uke's left arm with his right hand along the tatami to an angle of about 90 degrees from the body, while lifting his right leg over uke's body and placing his knee close to uke's left armpit (7, 8). Tori sits with his legs spread out over uke's body. The knees control uke's sides, and the toes are against the tatami. Tori's right hand continues its movement, touching the mat, circling uke's head (9) and takes

hold as deep as possible of uke's right lapel. In the grip, the thumb of the right hand is inside the lapel and the back of the hand points upwards (10, 11).

Tori executes the strangulation by leaning forward, pulling with the left hand and pushing slightly with the right hand (12, 13). Tori straightens the ankles while controlling uke's thighs with the soles of the feet. Simultaneously, tori squeezes uke's sides with the knees, further restricting uke's movement.

Uke tries to resist the stranglehold by pressing tori's elbows inwards with her hands and trying to bridge herself up on to her shoulders (12, 13). Uke's aim is to loosen the strangulation and release the grip. Tori

continues to choke and counters uke's defensive arms by leaning forward hard and forcefully over uke's head. Tori's forehead does not touch the mat. Realising that uke cannot block the choke, uke surrenders by tapping tori's body twice.

As uke surrenders, tori loosens the choke, stops briefly and releases the right hand grip from uke's lapel. Then tori lifts the right knee back over uke while pulling with the right hand uke's left arm back to uke's side and stands up straight in a kneeling position (14, 15).

Tori then releases the left hand grip and moves uke's right arm back into place (16). Finally, tori retreats to the chikama and opens kyoshi (17)

! Tori must control uke with the whole body. The knees must squeeze uke's sides, and the feet must be against uke's thighs (13). Foot control helps tori to keep his own balance. In the choke, the outer edge of the right hand and the wrist bone press against uke's neck. The thumb joint of the left hand presses on the other side. The wrists must not be turned so that the softer parts of the wrists are used for the choke.

Sometimes the right hand was first used to lift uke's left lapel up and only then insert the left hand into uke's left lapel. This is now considered an unnecessary movement.

In the past, it was also taught that tori would push the feet under uke's thighs. If there is a significant size difference between the couple, this is also a possible option, as long as control is maintained.

✱ To be successful, uke must make the escape attempt early enough and before tori gets a chance to lean the body weight forward. Uke should first try to loosen the choke and then try to push tori's right arm off (18, 19).

HADAKA-JIME Hadaka-jime is a "naked strangle". The name "hadaka" refers to the fact that the strangle is done without taking a hold of uke's judogi. In the katame-no-kata two versions of the strangle have been used; in the present one the hands are connected to each other at the left front side of uke's neck. In the second version, tori's right hand is placed in front of uke's throat connecting with tori's left elbow joint, and tori then slides his left hand behind uke's neck.

Hadaka-jime is also used in kime-no-kata, ju-no-kata and Kodokan goshin-jutsu.

PRINCIPLE
Tori's principle is to apply the choke with bare hands from behind on uke's trachea and to hold uke in a position where defending is very difficult.

TEACHING
Tori learns to make a technically correct choke and to control uke.

Uke learns one way to counter hadaka-jime. He learns how to loosen tori's right-hand grip by pulling down with both hands and pressing his chin into the resulting gap.

IMPORTANT
Tori's head and shoulder control over uke.

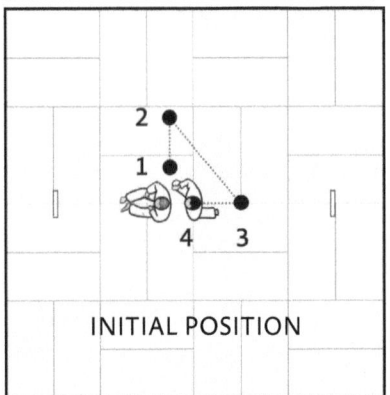

INITIAL POSITION

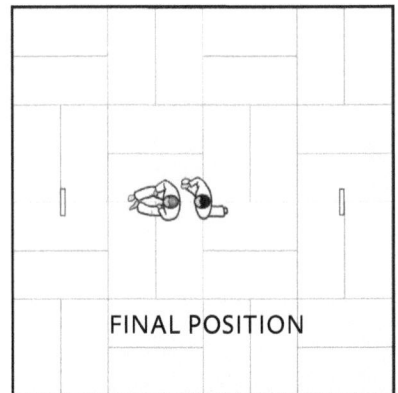

FINAL POSITION

EXECUTION

Tori retreats to the toma, opens kyoshi, stands up and moves towards the toma behind uke's head (1). As tori moves, uke sits up, straightens his back, slides his hands on his thighs, bends his left knee to place the sole of his left foot on the mat near his right ankle, and slightly bends his right knee (1). With uke now sitting, tori's toma is at a different place than in kami-shiho-gatame. If uke rises early enough, tori knows where to walk. Tori descends down, opens kyoshi (2), closes kyoshi and moves with two shikkos to the chikama and opens kyoshi (3).

Tori takes a short step to approach uke and comes close to uke's back (4). His right foot is just outside uke's hip, and his knee is slightly away from uke's back. Tori simultaneously brings his head and both hands over uke's shoulders, staying close to uke's neck. Tori slides his right hand under uke's chin and places his wrist against uke's throat (5). Tori's left wrist is on uke's shoulder. He joins his hands together. Right hand is on top. The palms only come halfway overlapping, so that the wrist is more in line with uke's neck. Tori presses his head against the side of uke's head and brings his shoulder forwards to control the back of uke's head (6). Tori can bring the strangling hand right up to uke's chin. When done this way, the hadaka-jime blocks the breath. The mechanism is the same as when swallowing, where the windpipe closes for a moment. Another possibility is to bring the hand over the windpipe, in which case the strangle is more of a painful strangle. In both cases there is an element of risk. When tori brings his hand under uke's chin, he may, by using

excessive force, break uke's hyoid bone or cause damage to the thyroid cartilage in the larynx. This is indicated by severe pain. In the other case, tori can crush uke's windpipe. In adults, the pain is so severe that the risk of this happening is low if surrender is immediate.

Starting with his left foot, tori moves his legs slightly backwards and then tightens his grip (6-10). Tori pulls uke backwards to an inclined position and lightly against his right knee. Uke's head is a bit tilted forward. Uke's head is slightly tilted forward. Tori's knee is touching approximately at uke's right shoulder blade. At the same time, tori keeps his right shoulder in contact with the back of uke's head. In this position, it's harder for uke to push or throw tori. The ball of tori's left foot stays in contact with the mat throughout.

Once tori has started to choke, uke will try to defend himself. Uke takes hold with his right hand on tori's right upper arm and with his left hand of tori's right elbow (8). Uke jerks with his hands downwards two or three times and tries to sneak his chin under tori's elbow. Finally, tori tightens the stranglehold by pulling further with his hands straight backwards, and uke is forced to surrender. Tori strangles uke in a controlled manner, mainly through movement backwards, rather than with the hands. Uke surrenders by tapping twice with the sole of his foot on the tatami (8).

After uke's surrender, tori loosens the stranglehold, brings his feet forward and releases his grip (11). Tori retreats backwards to the chikama without taking support with his hands from uke and opens kyoshi.

! Tori brings his arms and head over uke's shoulder line simultaneously to secure control of uke's head before he can react. Tori must make kuzushi before the choke. In this way he weakens uke's ability to defend himself.

Tori must have with his wrists, head and shoulder a good control of uke. He must bring his head in contact with uke's head to prevent him from turning his head for the escape. Tori must maintain a good balance at all times and be careful not to squeeze uke's windpipe too hard. Care must also be taken not to push uke's head too far forward with the shoulder, as there is a risk of neck lock.

In the past, the choke has also been done with the knee in the middle of uke's back and the surrender was made by hand tapping. Nowadays the knee is behind the right shoulder blade and the surrender signal is given with the foot.

✻ In trying to escape, uke tries to lose tori's grip on her throat, turns her head to the right and presses her chin against the elbow of tori, taking the power out of the choke (12, 13).

OKURI-ERI-JIME   Okuri-eri-jime's name in English is "sliding lapel strangle". The name may derive from the fact that, when the choke is applied, the lapels are slid or pulled in different directions. Okuri-eri-jime is also found in kime-no-kata, where tori's head controls uke's neck.

PRINCIPLE

The principle of the strangle is to take advantage of the lapels of uke's judogi to squeeze the blood vessels in the neck. At the same time, uke is held in a position, where defending is as difficult as possible. When performed correctly the choke does not target uke's trachea.

TEACHING

Okuri-eri-jime teaches tori the technically correct execution of the choke and control of uke during the execution.

Uke learns one way of trying to escape. In randori, tori is often behind uke, so tori has to control uke with his legs as well. Because tori straightens his arms in the choke, uke has to try to move up towards tori's head while trying to loosen the grip.

IMPORTANT

The position of tori's hands and the directions of the arm movements during the choke.

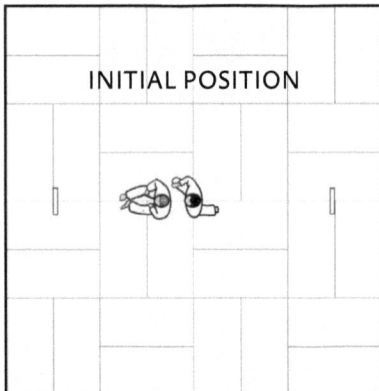
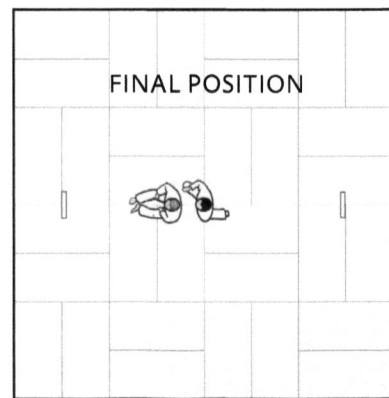

INITIAL POSITION   FINAL POSITION

EXECUTION

Tori approaches with a small step from the chikama close to uke's back (1), slips his left hand under uke's left armpit and grabs uke's left lapel at such a height that his right hand can still take grip of the lapel above it (2). Tori straightens the lapel by pulling it downwards. Then he reaches out with his right hand and puts his right hand over uke's right shoulder along the neck and takes a normal grip of the top of uke's left lapel (3). The grip is correct when the sharp edge of the wrist presses against the muscle of the neck.

Tori changes the grip of his left hand to a normal grip on uke's right lapel as high up as possible, places his head on the left side of uke's head and controls uke's body by pressing his right shoulder against the back side of uke's head (4). Starting with his left foot, tori moves slightly backwards and unbalances uke (5). Tori's right knee lightly supports uke's back and controls uke's body from the right side. Uke is more against tori's right thigh than in hadaka-jime.

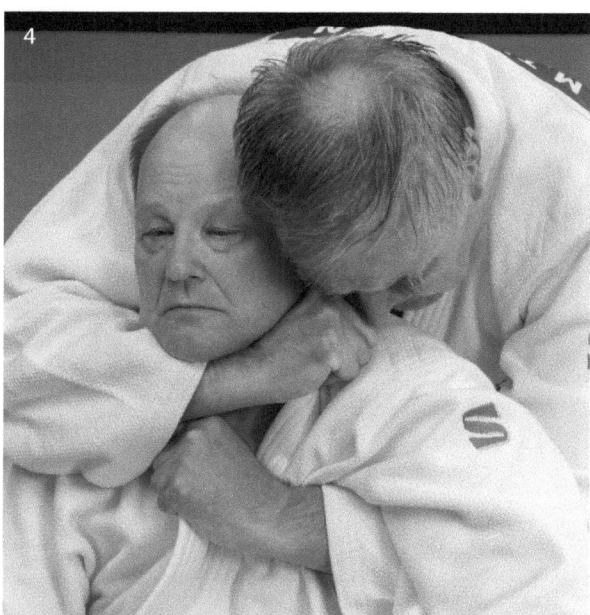

Tori executes the strangle by straightening his arms. The hands act as if they were an extension of the lapel. The left hand pulls the lapel downwards and the right hand pulls to the right. Tori's grip tightens as he moves backwards. There is a small body rotation to the right in the choke. (5–8).

Uke tries to defend himself in the same way as in hadaka-jime (7, 8). After realising that he cannot escape, uke surrenders by tapping his foot twice on the tatami.

After uke surrenders, tori loosens the choke, moves his legs closer to uke (9) and releases his grip. Tori retreats backwards to the chikama without taking support with his hands from uke and opens kyoshi (10).

! The chokes from behind follow each other fairly quickly. Tori must clearly retreat to the chikama, wait a moment and then go in for another choke. Tori must make kuzushi before the choke. He must have good control of uke throughout the choke. Balance must be maintained.

The ball of the left foot must be against the tatami at all times, the head must be controlled and the shoulder should control the back of uke's head. All these are elements the absence of which are considered mistakes.

In the past, it was customary to pull uke's left lapel outwards at first and grab it with the right hand. Nowadays it is sufficient to tighten the lapel down just enough to allow the thumb of the right hand to slide in between the neck and lapel and grip the lapel.

In some older kata books, tori is not advised to move backwards. Some have shown control of uke's head by tori pressing with the top of his head against uke's neck like in kime-no-kata.

* Like in hadaka-jime, uke tries to escape by loosening tori's stranglehold using both hands and pressing her chin against the crook of tori's elbow to make the strangulation ineffective (11, 12).

KATAHA-JIME The name "single wing strangle" refers to the way in which the choke is made. One of uke's hands is brought into a position that resembles a bird's wing drawn backwards. Kataha-jime is also used in kime-no-kata, where it is done in a slightly different manner.

PRINCIPLE

The principle of this strangle from behind is that the blood vessels to uke's head are blocked by applying pressure on the muscles of the neck. From the right side of uke's neck the pressure is caused by the hand and from the left side with uke's own lapel. At the same time uke is kept in a position where it is as difficult as possible to defend himself. When performed correctly, the strangle has little or no effect on uke's trachea.

TEACHING

Kataha-jime teaches tori the technically correct strangle and the control needed. In randori, the strangle is typically done lying on one side or on the back, in which case tori has to control uke with his legs as well.

It teaches uke one way to counter the choke by blocking tori from putting his left arm behind uke's neck.

IMPORTANT

The placement of tori's right hand on uke's lapel and the movement of tori's left hand behind uke's head.

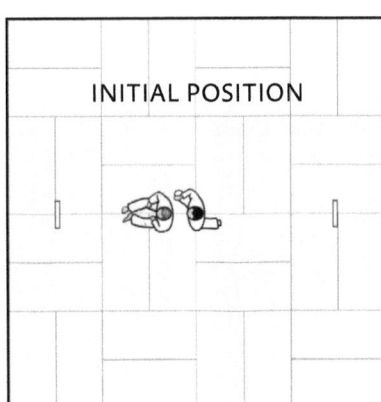

INITIAL POSITION

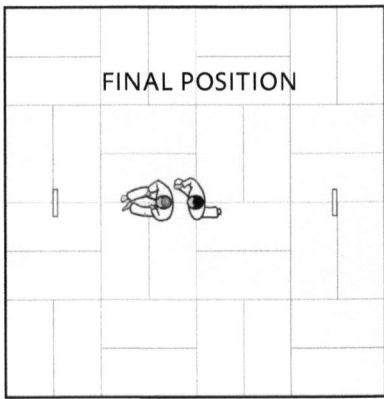

FINAL POSITION

EXECUTION

Tori moves from the chikama close to uke's back (1).

Tori grabs uke's left lapel in the same way as in okuri-eri-jime (2). Then he takes with his right hand in front of uke's throat a normal grip of uke's left lapel (3). The grip is not so high up at the lapel as in okuri-eri-jime. The place of the strangling hand should be found so that the choke is directed towards the muscles on the right side of uke's neck, not the trachea.

Tori moves his left forearm to uke's left elbow bend, then pulls the hand first to the left (4) and then up. The palm is towards himself. At the same time, tori straightens his stance.

When uke's hand is upright (5), tori continues the motion and pushes his left hand, wrist stiff, behind uke's neck and under his own right hand (6, 7). Tori moves his right foot further to the side, turns his toes to the right and unbalances uke backwards lightly against his own thigh (8). Due to the rotation, uke is resting nearly on his tailbone.

Uke tries to escape by grabbing with his right hand his own left wrist and pulling his arms forcefully downwards (7, 8).

Tori continues to choke by twisting more to the right, pushing his left arm further down under his right arm and pulling with his right hand. Tori should try to pull with his right hand, as if the hand is an extension of the lapel. Uke is tilted backwards and slightly to the right. Tori controls uke's right side against his right thigh. Finding that he cannot escape, uke surrenders by tapping the tatami twice with his foot.

As uke surrenders, tori loosens the choke and brings uke upright, then brings his foot closer to uke and releases his grip.

Tori retreats to the chikama without taking support with his hands from uke and opens kyoshi (9).

! Tori must find a suitable distance for the initial position from which the movements can be done without taking an extra step back with the left foot. Uke's left hand must be brought to the side so that he cannot resist the lifting action so well. In addition, tori must be in good control of the backwards leaning uke, and he must maintain his balance throughout the choke.

In the past, there has also been a version where tori brings his left hand behind uke's neck in a kime-no-kata style. Another, totally different version, shows uke attempting to throw tori forward by raising his own left arm and reaching for tori's neck. Uke tries to grab with his right hand tori's lapel and pull tori over himself. Tori uses the situation and slips his left hand in front of uke's hand and then behind his neck.

* In randori, uke has to make the escape much earlier and block tori from raising uke's left arm up to prevent tori from bringing her hand behind uke's neck. Once the lift is blocked, uke can try to break tori's balance and get into a better position to counter the choke.

Uke's aim is to pull tori's left hand down and away from behind her neck. Depending on tori's balance, uke may attempt to roll her over (10, 11).

GYAKU-JUJI-JIME Gyaku-juji-jime belongs to the cross strangles. The "gyaku" as "inverted" in its name refers to the fact that the hands are the other way round than in nami-juji-jime. Like other cross-strangles, gyaku-juji-jime is a very effective strangle when combined with a variety of roll overs and turns.

PRINCIPLE

The principle of this strangle is to block the blood flow to the head by pressing neck muscles with the hands. The kata also sets out the principle of how the strangle can be continued after uke has blocked the first attempt. When performed correctly, the strangle has little or no effect on uke's trachea.

TEACHING

When learning gyaku-juji-jime, tori learns the technically correct way of strangling and how to continue the situation after uke's block.

Uke learns one possible way to counter the choke. In randori uke must try to block the choke as early as possible.

IMPORTANT

The position of tori's hands on uke's lapels and the direction of the pull in the strangle. In addition, tori must have good control of uke's legs.

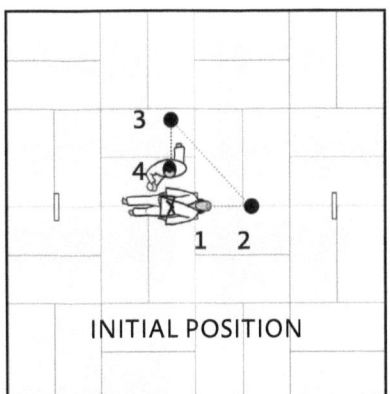

INITIAL POSITION

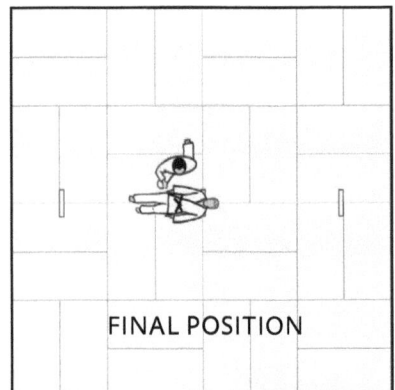

FINAL POSITION

Execution

Tori retreats from the chikama to the toma, opens kyoshi and stands up. He then moves to uke's right side to the toma. As tori walks, uke goes into a supine position (1). In the toma, tori descends down, opens kyoshi, moves with two shikkos to the chikama and opens kyoshi.

Tori takes an approach step from chikama and moves uke's right arm to his own left side in the same manner as in kata-juji-jime (2).

Continuing the same way, tori takes with his left hand a grip of uke's left lapel (3), moves uke's left arm with his right hand to the side and straddles on uke's body (4). Knees control uke's sides and can be slightly further away from the armpits than in kata-juji-jime. The toes are against the tatami. Tori pushes his right hand palm upwards from above his left hand deep into uke's right lapel (5). The fingers are inside the lapels and the thumbs on the outside.

Tori tightens the stranglehold by leaning forward on top of uke and pulling with both hands (6).

Uke tries to defend himself and loosen the stranglehold by placing his palms on Tori's elbows and twisting hands clockwise, viewed from the direction of uke. He pushes with his left hand tori's right elbow upwards and with his right hand, presses tori's left elbow downwards and raises his hips upwards (7). Uke's elbows should be in line with the direction of the pushes. Uke must start defending immediately after the stranglehold is applied and before the strangulation is completely tight.

Tori falls on his left side, thus preventing uke's escape attempt. Due to uke's push, tori's head comes slightly higher than uke's head (8). Tori's legs are still around uke.

Tori crosses his legs and tightens the stranglehold by pulling his arms towards his stomach (9). Uke tries still to defend himself by pressing on tori's elbows but fails and surrenders by tapping with his left hand on tori.

As uke surrenders, tori loosens the choke, after which both of them turn back together to the initial position of the strangle (10). Tori still holds hands on uke's lapels (11). While turning back uke can subtly support tori.

Tori releases his right hand from uke's lapel and returns it to his original position in exactly the same way as in kata-juji-jime (12–15). After lifting uke's right arm back to uke's right side, tori can, if necessary, discreetly pull uke to the right spot if he has moved.

Tori retreats to the chikama and opens kyoshi (16).

! When tori falls to the side, he must remain on his left side, so that uke's right hand remains under uke. Tori can also lightly push with his right foot to make it easier to fall. At the end of the strangle, tori controls uke between his legs, but not squeezing uke with them. Tori should use his hands as an extension of the lapel. The sharp edges of the hands should be held against uke's neck.

In the past, it has been taught that uke takes tori down. Nowadays, uke is taken down by tori and too much activity on the part of uke is considered a mistake.

In the early versions of the katame-no-kata, tori's left hand was on the top of the right hand in the strangle. In this case, the roll was also performed in the other direction i.e. to the right, looking from tori.

In the past, it was advised to lift with the right hand, like in the kata-juji-jime, uke's left lapel up to tension before the left hand is pushed into the lapel. In addition, it has also been done in such a way that tori fell totally on his back and he was not allowed to cross his legs.

16

* Uke first tries to loosen the stranglehold and then release tori's right hand grip. She can then continue with, for example, by pushing tori to her right side (17, 18).

ADJUSTING THE JUDOGI

After shime-waza

Tori retreats to the toma, opens kyoshi, stands up, moves to the side of uke's head to his starting position, descends down and opens kyoshi. While tori moves to his position, uke first rises to a sitting position and then he rises into a kyoshi. The movements should be timed so that both open kyoshi at the same time.

Tori and uke adjust their judogis with simultaneous movements and stop for a moment.

The shime-waza is completed.

KANSETSU-WAZA

The power of the arm locks is based on the pain caused when the elbow joint is bent into a hyperextension or twisting the hand in an angle. The pain is caused by stretching of the ligaments and increased pressure in the synovial sac. The last technique in the kata called ashi-garami is a lock made to the knee. This technique, originally allowed in competitions is dangerous, as the pain in the knee is often not felt until the joint is already damaged.

As with chokes, locks are not successful unless tori first controls uke and especially his shoulder area. To do this, he uses his whole body and limbs. In this way, tori prevents uke from turning into a position where the lock is no longer effective. The bending of the limb with only the hands rarely produces the desired result. Many lock techniques must be done in exactly the right direction to work.

Kansetsu-waza techniques are UDE-GARAMI (1), UDE-HISHIGI-JUJI-GATAME (2), UDE-HISHIGI-UDE-GATAME (3), HIZA-GATAME (4) and ASHI-GARAMI (5).

Uke's attacks and tori's lock techniques occur in kansetsu-waza relatively quickly. The lock must be technically clean and effective (6, 7). Again, the most important thing is to present the principle. Locks work differently for different people. It is particularly difficult to do an arm lock to a person with hyper-mobile joints. Tori and uke should examine the position in which the lock is most effective. In training, one should avoid tightening the lock every time to the point of pain. Locks should be practised one at a time and the escapes to the end in between. Uke can vary different escapes, so that tori better understands the meaning of his own movements. In all arm locks and especially in ashi-garami, care must be taken.

Movements should be well rhythmical, clearly perceptible and well-timed. It is not only the outcome that is important, but also the movements and control used to achieve it.

Uke tries to defend himself in all lock situations. This is often not very obvious, because the kata is supposed to show how the lock is made and uke's defence is practically overdue. In randori, uke can react with the same defensive moves at an earlier stage.

7

UDE-GARAMI   Ude-garami means an arm entangling arm lock. A similar lock is also found in ju-no-kata and Kodokan goshin-jutsu.

PRINCIPLE

Tori's principle in ude-garami is to control uke from the side and to execute a garami lock in this situation. Tori controls uke with his upper body, hands and legs.

TEACHING

Tori learns to quickly take ude-garami grip and to perform a technically correct execution.

By studying ude-garami, uke learns to understand in which situation the lock occurs and how it could have been avoided.

IMPORTANT

Tori must get uke's hand and upper body under control early enough.

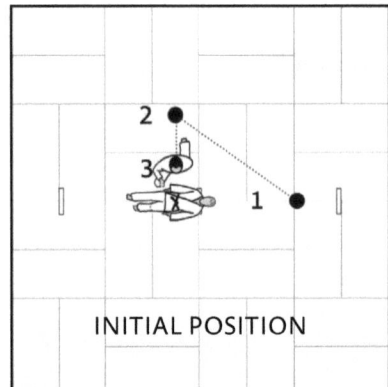

INITIAL POSITION

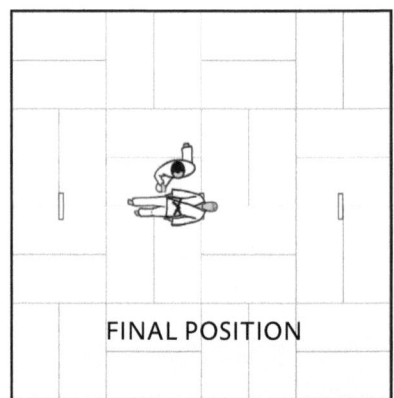

FINAL POSITION

EXECUTION

After the judogi adjustment, uke goes into a supine position in the same way and in the same place as before. Once uke has gone onto his back, tori stands up, walks to uke's right side to the toma, lowers himself into kyoshi and opens it (1). Then tori moves with two shikkos to the chikama and opens kyoshi.

Tori takes an approach step from the chikama forward (2) and raises uke's right arm to his left side as in the kesa-gatame (3).

Tori places his right hand on uke's right armpit, presses with his thumb lightly uke's shoulder to the mat and moves his left knee to uke's armpit (3). Tori releases his grip on uke's hand and straightens his back (4). He then indicates his intention to attack by making a small nod and at the same time turning his gaze towards uke (5). This is a signal for uke to start attacking.

Uke tries to grab tori's right lapel with his left hand (6), perhaps with the intention of pulling tori over him onto the tatami. In the attack uke lifts his left shoulder off the mat. Uke's attack does not have to be particularly fast, but it must be powerful. The upper body should also be used.

Tori prevents uke from grabbing by bringing the edge of his left palm in front of uke's hand (6). The thumb is downwards and on a different side of uke's arm than the fingers. Tori slides his hand along uke's forearm up to his wrist, pushing uke's arm away and down towards the tatami (7) and grabs uke's wrist. He lowers his right knee to the mat, drops down on uke's chest and spreads out his knees to uke's right side. The position of the legs should be wide and sturdy. At the same time, tori brings his right arm from under uke's arm to his own left wrist and takes the ude-garami grip (8). Tori presses uke's arm onto the tatami straight to the side. The angle between uke's upper arm and forearm is already almost 90 degrees when the arm hits the mat.

Tori does the ude-garami by pulling with both hands uke's arm to a right angle close to uke's left side, twisting uke's wrist outwards and lifting uke's elbow slightly upwards (9). Tori does not lift his right shoulder. He must control with his knees and his chest uke's body so that uke cannot turn to the right.

Uke tries to resist the lock by turning his wrist inwards and by lifting his left shoulder and hips up (9). Tori counters the attempt by holding uke on his back. Uke surrenders by tapping twice with his free hand on tori's body.

Once uke has surrendered, tori immediately releases the lock and holds this position for a short moment. Then pulling lightly with his right hand he returns uke's left arm to uke's left side. After rising to a kneeling position, tori returns uke's right arm to its original position.

Tori retreats to the chikama and opens kyoshi.

! Tori's grips on his own and uke's wrist must be strong. Thumb and fingers must be on different sides of the wrist, otherwise the grip can slip. The grip on uke's wrist must be taken early on before the wrist is on the tatami.

All movements are important when doing the lock. It is not enough for tori to just lift uke's elbow.

In the past, it was taught that uke's attack occurred immediately when tori had moved uke's right arm to the side. Nowadays tori shows his intention to attack with a small nod.

Ude-garami has been done also in the way that tori presses uke's hand well above uke's shoulder line and then onto the mat.

* In randori, uke must try to escape the lock as early as possible. Uke may try to grab her own left wrist with her right hand (10), lift her left shoulder and hip off the mat, and try to turn to the right (11). If tori's control over uke's body and her left elbow are poor, it is also possible for uke to pull the elbow inwards and turn left.

UDE-HISHIGI-JUJI-GATAME Ude-hishigi-juji-gatame or juji-gatame is a very effective and the most common lock used in competitions. Most arm locks have the additional words ude-hishigi at the beginning. These words mean an arm crushing or dislocating an arm. This was the original purpose of arm locks. In addition, the term ude-hishigi has helped to clarify that it is an arm lock and not a hold-down. This clarification is particularly necessary for names containing the word gatame (to hold, to control). Juji (cross) refers to the straight alignment between tori and uke.

PRINCIPLE
Tori's principle is to completely control uke with ankles, thighs and hands and do the lock by lifting his own hips.

TEACHING
Tori learns to quickly take control of uke's arm and to hold the control until the lock is effective. Tori controls uke's right arm between his thighs and uke's upper body with his legs. At the same time, tori learns how to execute a technically correct lock.

Juji-gatame teaches uke one possible escape. In randori, uke must try to block the lock before the arm is straight.

IMPORTANT
Tori must have control over uke's arm at all times when he sits down.

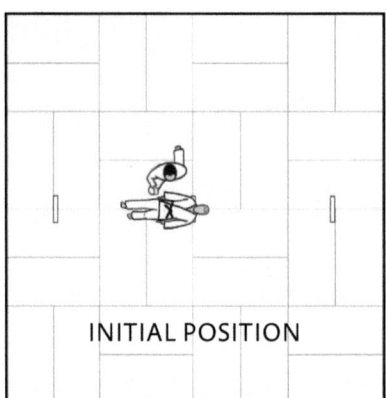

INITIAL POSITION

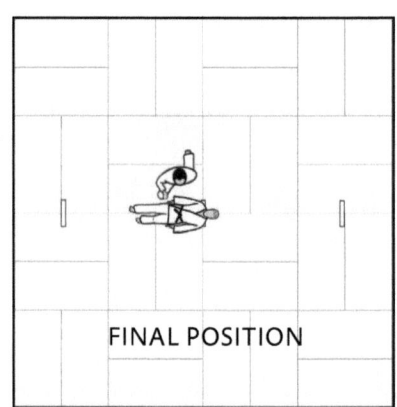

FINAL POSITION

EXECUTION

Tori moves slightly closer to uke from the chikama. As he approaches, he moves directly towards uke in the same way as in the other techniques (1).

Tori signals his intention to attack with a slight nod of the head.

Uke tries to reach out with his right hand to grab a grip of tori's left lapel (2). When reaching out, uke's right shoulder comes off the mat.

Before uke can get a grip, tori grabs uke's wrist with his right hand and immediately also with his left hand below the right hand. Tori pulls with both hands on uke's arm slightly upwards and presses uke's wrist against his own chest. Then he pushes toes of his right foot deep under uke's armpit (3), leans his upper body forward and controls uke with the shin of his right leg. Keeping his weight on his right leg, tori brings his left foot in an arc around uke's head and places the sole of his foot on the tatami so that his achilles tendon is against the side of uke's neck (4, 5).

Tori clamps uke's right upper arm between his thighs (5), lowers himself close to his own right heel (5), and then rolls onto his back perpendicular to uke (6). While going to the supine position, tori should be careful and allow uke to rise a little from the mat to avoid injury to the arm. Tori goes on his back with his back slightly rounded.

Tori locks uke's elbow by firmly holding uke's arm against his chest, squeezing his thighs together and lifting his hips up. Tori's head should be off the mat (7, 8).

Uke tries to escape by bridging on his shoulders, turning his body over his left shoulder, and at the same time pulling his right arm free (8). Tori raises

his hips a little more, causing the lock to take more effect and uke surrenders by tapping twice on tori's leg.

Once uke has surrendered, tori releases the lock and pauses briefly. Uke then moves to align with the kata-axis. Tori turns in coordination with uke, maintaining a hold on uke's right arm. Standing upright without taking support from the tatami, tori may, for example, move the left foot next to uke's head, push off the tatami to slide further away from uke, bend the left knee sideways in front, and rise onto the left knee (9). Tori then adjusts the kneeling position slightly to the right. Finally, uke's arm is returned to its original position.

Tori returns to the chikama and opens kyoshi (10).

! In juji-gatame, it is essential that tori keeps his knees close together and uke's arm between his thighs. Tori's right foot should be under uke's right shoulder, the left heel on the mat and the ankle controlling uke's neck. When the toes are turned slightly inwards, tori can press his thighs together more easily. Tori keeps with the pull of both hands uke's right arm straight and presses uke's wrist and his little finger towards tori's chest. If uke is able to turn very far in the escape attempt it is a sign of poor control.

If uke has moved from his starting position after the arm has been returned, tori can use his hands to guide uke to the correct place.

Sometimes tori has done a small turn of his body to the right to ensure that uke does not escape. However, in kata competitions this may be seen as an extra movement and an indication of lack of control.

✱ Uke can escape by turning counter-clockwise early enough and assuming an all-fours position. (11, 12).

UDE-HISHIGI-UDE-GATAME

Ude-gatame is an arm lock done to a straightened arm, in which uke's wrist being one of the fulcrum points. Usually the wrist is against tori's neck or shoulder. In the original version of the ude-gatame, tori pressed uke's arm with his right forearm. In the early versions, uke had taken a grip on tori's lapel. Ude-gatame is also found in Kodokan goshin-jutsu.

PRINCIPLE

Tori's principle is to control uke's body, arm, and wrist in a posture, in which he can pull his hands towards himself and lock uke's straight arm.

TEACHING

Ude-gatame teaches tori to take control over uke's arm quickly using his neck and hands and hold the arm until a technically correct lock is effective. At the same time it teaches tori to control uke with his right knee so that uke cannot turn or rise up.

Ude-gatame teaches uke one possible escape from this lock. In randori uke must try to block the lock before tori can straighten uke's arm against his neck. Uke can either push his arm further away and bend it, or pull his hand downwards away from tori's neck.

IMPORTANT

Tori's control with the neck, shoulder and right hand from uke's wrist precedes the control with both hands.

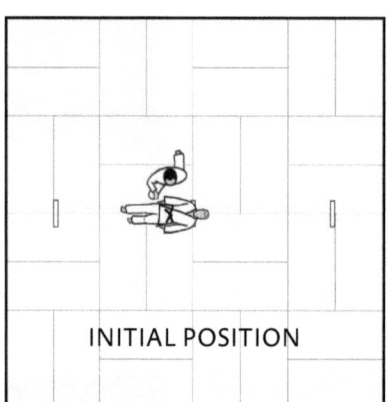

INITIAL POSITION

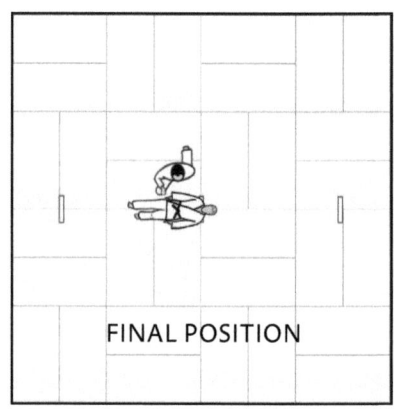

FINAL POSITION

EXECUTION

Tori moves slightly forward from the chikama (1) and moves uke's arm to tori's left side in the same way as in ude-garami (2). When tori has released his grip from uke's arm he straightens up and indicates with a small nod his intention to attack (3, 4).

Uke reaches up and tries to grab tori's right upper lapel with his left hand (4). Maybe uke's aim is to pull tori over him. In reaching for the grip, uke's left shoulder comes off the mat.

Tori leans a little more forward, tilts his head to the right, locks uke's wrist between his shoulder and neck and brings his right palm onto uke's elbow (5). Tori presses uke's hand with his right hand against his neck, brings his left palm on top of his right hand and presses his right shin against uke's lower ribs, preventing uke from rising (6). Tori straightens his body, thereby stretching uke's elbow joint. He rotates his palms slightly counterclockwise, tightening control over uke's arm. At the same time, tori turns his upper body slightly to the left and tightens the lock by pulling uke's elbow towards himself and lifting up slightly (8). The last lifting movement is quite small.

Tori can intensify the movement by pressing on uke's elbow upwards on the side of his little finger at the end (8).

Uke tries to counter the lock by pulling his arm downwards but is unable to escape, and surrenders by tapping his hand twice on uke's body. The move in uke's escape attempt is very small. However, it is worth testing occasionally, that tori's control is real.

Once uke has surrendered, tori releases the lock and guides uke's left arm back to its place with his right hand (9). He then uses both hands to return uke's right arm to its place (10). Tori retreats to the chikama and opens kyoshi.

! Tori's right knee prevents uke from turning to the right and from rising too much. This control must also be visible. Tori's posture should be as sturdy as possible.

If tori's control of uke with the right foot is poor, uke may also try to escape by coming closer to tori and bending the arm. In kata, uke will attempt to pull the arm downwards.

* Uke's escape is to pull the arm down early enough and get the wrist out from tori's neck (11, 12).

UDE-HISHIGI-HIZA-GATAME The last two techniques of katame-no-kata differ from the others in that they also show the situation from which the final lock is reached. The name hiza-gatame comes from the fact that the force of the lock comes from tori's knee, which presses uke's arm into the lock. According to the Kodokan definition, the hiza-gatame locks also include those techniques in which the hand is pressed or bent against the knee. Originally, this technique was performed from the left-sided kyoshi as a mirror image.

PRINCIPLE
In hiza-gatame of katame-no-kata, tori's principle is to make uke fall from the initial position into one where tori can control uke with his feet and hands and execute the lock by pressing uke's elbow down with his knee.

TEACHING
Tori learns to take control of uke and to perform hiza-gatame quickly and technically correctly. At the same time he learns which direction and how the knee must be pressed to apply pressure and make the lock as effective as possible.

Hiza-gatame teaches uke one possible escape. The escape can be attempted either by pushing the hand in tori's armpit further or by pulling it away. In kata, uke tries to push forward.

IMPORTANT
Tori must keep uke under control all the time while he falls uke to the tatami.

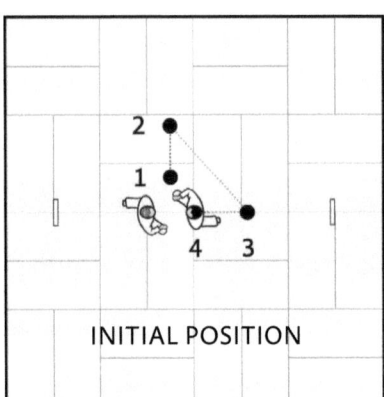

INITIAL POSITION

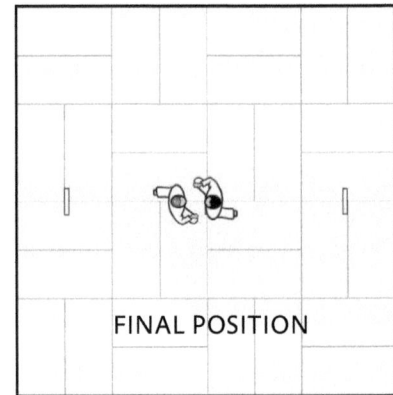

FINAL POSITION

EXECUTION

Tori retreats with two shikko steps to the toma and opens kyoshi. He then stands up, moves to the to the side uke's head to the toma, descends down and opens kyoshi. At the same time, uke stands up to kyoshi in the same way as for adjustment of judogis (1).

Tori takes two shikko steps forward and opens kyoshi (2). Then both take an approach step (3). The approach step is similar as when tori approaches uke from the chikama.

Tori and uke take the normal right handed grip (4).

Tori releases his left hand from uke's right upper arm, takes it from below and inside around uke's hand (5) and takes a grip with an open palm of uke's elbow. Tori squeezes uke's wrist into his own armpit (6).

Tori breaks uke's balance forward, lifts the sole of his right foot to uke's left groin and falls on his right side

(7, 8). During the fall, tori places the sole of his left foot on uke's hip on his back (10). The sole of the foot is approximately at uke's belt. Tori should not fall too much back or too far away. Uke will fall on his knees next to tori.

After falling to the mat, uke tries to escape by leaning his body forward and pushing his right hand deeper into tori's armpit (10). Uke's attempt is to, for

example, bend his arm and get a hold-down of tori. When tipping uke over, tori must be careful not to push too hard with his feet and causing uke to land on his stomach. Uke must be on his knees so that the lock will be successful.

Tori counters uke's attempt by pushing with his legs uke further away while squeezing with his upper arm uke's wrist more firmly into his armpit. Tori's right hand prevents uke from retreating further away.

Tori does the lock by turning uke's elbow clockwise and pressing with his left knee and his hand downwards (11).

When realizing that the lock is effective, uke surrenders by tapping twice on the tatami with his hand. Tori immediately loosens the lock. Both then get up on their knees and open kyoshi at the same spot, where hiza-gatame began (12). Opening kyoshi is good to be timed to happen at the same time.

! Tori's left hand grip should be from uke's right elbow joint and not from the fabric. The hand helps tori know where uke's elbow is so that he can align his knee correctly. Tori needs to set the right foot on uke's groin and not on the knee. If the foot is in the knee, uke will easily fall on his stomach, leg control will be poor and the effect of the lock is poor. If there is a big difference in size between the pair, it can be difficult for tori to get his feet in just the right places. The key is to get the bodies in a position, where tori can press uke's elbow with his knee properly.

In the past, it has been taught that tori takes grip with his left hand just above uke's elbow. It has also been possible to grab the sleeve. Nowadays, the teaching is to grab the elbow. Sometimes it has been taught to place the knee directly against uke's elbow.

* For the escape, uke must push the arm far enough to bend the elbow (13, 14). This is only possible if it is done early enough or if tori's feet control of uke is poor.

ASHI-GARAMI　Ashi-garami is a knee lock modified to fit the kata. Garami refers to the wrapping. The take down shown in the kata is originally a jujutsu technique. The lock is preserved in katame-no-kata as a reminder of the roots of judo and the effectiveness of leg locks. Use of knee locks in judo competitions was banned in 1916. The second leg lock in judo kata can be found in Kodokan goshin-jutsu (mae-geri).

PRINCIPLE

Tori's principle in ashi-garami is to wrap the left leg around uke's right leg and control uke with both hands and the right foot. Tori does the lock by straightening the left leg.

TEACHING

Tori learns to perform ashi-garami technically correctly. In ashi-garami, tori forces uke's leg to bend sideways. Since the knee does not sense pain in the same way as the elbow, tori and uke must be particularly careful with this lock. The speed should only be added to the execution once the technical components are in place.

For uke, ashi-garami teaches one (theoretical) escape. While standing, uke still has the opportunity to avoid the lock by pressing his knee on tori's stomach and turning to the left. Escaping on the mat is only possible if tori's control of uke with his right foot and hands is poor. In this case, uke must turn to the left and bend his knee. It is not advisable to do any sudden strong movements, as the risk of injury is high.

IMPORTANT

Tori must be able to slip his left leg around uke's right leg and get uke to fall over.

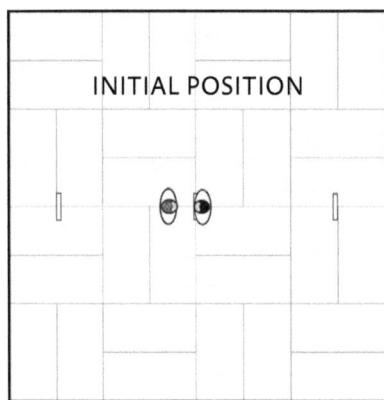

INITIAL POSITION

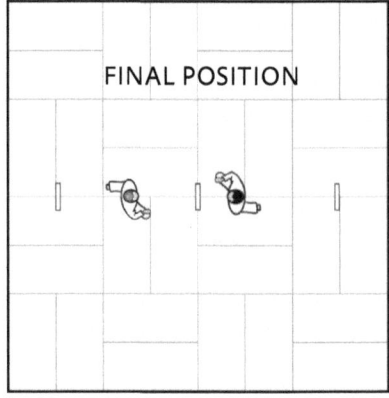

FINAL POSITION

EXECUTION

Tori and uke stand up at the same time, step half a step forward with their right foot and take a grip in migi-shizentai (1).

Tori steps between uke's legs with his left foot, breaks uke's balance forward with both hands (2)

and starts to do tomoe-nage by sacrificing himself and lifting the sole of his right foot to uke's lower abdomen (3, 4). The throw attempt must be real.

Uke blocks the attempted throw by taking a long step with his right foot forward (4).

When tori is on the mat, uke lifts tori directly upwards (5). Due to the lift, uke's weight is more on the right foot. Supporting on the left foot, tori slides the body under uke (6). At the same time, the sole of the right foot descends onto uke's knee (7), and uke is controlled with the hands. By pushing with the right foot and steering with the hands, tori pulls uke to bend forward while turning the body slightly to the right side. Then, the left foot encircles uke's right leg from the outside and moves under the stomach

(8). With the right foot, tori pushes uke by the knee and knocks uke down forward (9, 10). Uke performs a mae-ukemi on the left forearm. When uke falls, tori turns further to the right side.

In ashi-garami, there is variation in the point at which tori places the right foot on uke's knee. There is also variation in whether tori first encircles the leg and then knocks uke down, or waits until uke is about to fall or has already fallen (11).

Uke still tries to escape by turning left (12), but tori blocks this with the hands. Tori makes a lock by straightening the left leg, twisting the hips to the right and holding uke tight under control with the hands (13). Uke surrenders by tapping twice the tatami with the left hand.

Once uke has surrendered, tori immediately loosens the lock by slightly lifting the knee. Tori releases the grip and retreats about a metre on the mat backwards before rising into kyoshi. He can do this for example, by retreating with leaning on his hands and taking a couple of steps on all fours. This is because for the closing ceremonies tori must get to the right spot with two shikkos. Uke may also need to retreat a little before rising into kyoshi. Both have to move to the place where the next steps can be taken correctly.

Tori and uke should time their movements so that the back straightening and kyoshi opening take place at the same time.

! When performing the lock, tori controls uke with both hands and the right foot. The right hand grip from uke's lapel prevents uke from turning to the left, and the right foot prevents uke from coming closer. If the hand control is poor, uke's right foot is vertical and the toes point down. Then there is most likely no lock present, as uke can bend his leg and escape the lock.

In the past, the tomoe-nage attempt did not have to be real. Today, kuzushi is expected to be present and followed by an immediate sacrifice. When tori knocks uke down by pressing on uke's knee, uke has to do a mae-ukemi and also try to escape.

* For the escape, uke must turn left and try to get the knee bent (14, 15). However, particular care must be taken here, because the risk of injury is high.

CLOSING FORMALITIES

Tori and uke are facing each other in kyoshi. First, tori takes two shikko steps backwards to the position where he was after the opening step and opens kyoshi.

Then uke takes one shikko-step backwards to the position he was after the opening step and opens kyoshi.

After kansetzu-waza

ADJUSTING THE JUDOGI AND CLOSING

Tori and uke are now four metres apart. They adjust their judogis at the same time.

Tori and uke stand up simultaneously and take the closing step. Then they descend down and do a kneeling bow.

They stand up, turn to face the shomen, and perform a standing bow. Then, they turn towards each other, step back to the edge of the kata area, and perform another standing bow.

Katame-no-kata is completed.

THE EDITORIAL BOARD

PETER MICKELSSON (6th dan, b. 1958) is a retired chief editor. Peter started judo in 1973 and has been a judo teacher since 1980. He has previously served as the chairman for the Finnish Dan Holders Society and graduation committee for several years. Peter has seven individual judo Finnish championship medals. He has 30 medals at Finnish and Nordic kata championships and a place in kime-no-kata World Cup finals 2008. Peter holds Kodokan diplomas in Kodokan goshin-jutsu and itsutsu-no-kata. He is an international judge in Kodokan goshin-jutsu 2014 and ju-no-kata 2023. Peter is the other photographer of this book.

STAFFAN LINDGREN (6. dan, b. 1945) started judo in 1966. Staffan is the "grand old man" of Finnish judo. He is an A-level coach and A-level shiai judge, He has worked for decades both as a promoter and as a kata teacher at national level. Staffan founded Hontai Judo together with his wife Satu Lindgren in 1990 and served as the club's head instructor and president for more than 30 years. He was the first Finnish international kata judge back in 2005. Staffan holds the IJF judge licenses for all five competition katas since 2012. He has acted as head judge for the finals of numerous European Championships and World Championships. In addition, he has also acted as a member of Finnish kata commission since it was established.

HANNU MUSTONEN (6th dan, b. 1957) has practised judo continuously since 1970. He is a judo Finnish championship medallist. Hannu has served on the board of the Finnish Dan Holders Society and as a promoter at the national level. He is an active kata instructor and the head kata instructor for the Finnish Judo Association. Hannu is an IJF and EJU certified kata judge for all five competition katas. He has acted in many finals of European Championships and World Championship kata competitions as a head judge. Hannu has been a long time member of the kata commission of Finnish Judo Association.

JORMA PAASI (3.dan, b. 1954) is a retired M.Sc. of Technology who started his judo career in 1976. He has won a total of 15 medals in Nordic and Finnish kata championships. Jorma has been the chairman of the kata commission of Finnish Judo Association since 2017. He is also a national kata instructor and judge and he has published kata manuals on all five competition katas. He is also an award-winning nature photographer.

Background on the Photography

The technique photos in this book were taken at the Hontai Judo dojo between 2017 and 2023. With a few exceptions, the images capture full-speed kata executions, as this approach was essential to providing an authentic and realistic presentation of kata. While no kata is perfect, and despite the careful review by the panel of experts, minor technical inaccuracies may appear in the photos due to the nature of live-action photography.

The images on pages 14, 15, 16, 17, 18 and 19 are published "with the cooperation of Kodokan Judo Institute".

Photo on page 2 Keijo Saarelainen: Tori Jorma Paasi, uke Otso Koski.

Persons appearing in the technical photos (with dan grades at the time of publication):
Wolfgang Dax-Romswinkel, 8th dan, five-time World Champion in ju-no-kata
Ulla Loosen, 7th dan, five-time World Champion in ju-no-kata
Peter Mickelsson, 6th dan
Mikko Tuominen, 5th dan, katame-no-kata European Championship 3.
Samu Laitinen, 5th dan, katame-no-kata European Championship 3.
Pasi Oinas, 4th dan, nage-no-kata European Championship 3.
Mika Salsoila, 4th dan, nage-no-kata European Championship 3.
Jorma Paasi, 3rd dan, Kodokan goshin-jutsu Nordic Champion
Juha Turunen, 3rd dan, katame-no-kata Nordic Champion
Pekka Väyrynen, 3rd dan, katame-no-kata Nordic Champion
Jussi Nikander, 2nd dan, Kodokan goshin-jutsu Nordic Champion
Kati Stoyanov-Pitkänen, 2nd dan
Heli Vartiainen, 2nd dan
Otso Koski, 2nd dan

ACKNOWLEDGEMENTS

Many of Finland's leading kata experts contributed to the creation of this book. The editorial board included international kata judges Staffan Lindgren, Peter Mickelsson and Hannu Mustonen. Their extensive judo and kata knowledge and their active involvement were irreplaceable in both writing the text and in shooting the photos. Special thanks to them for this! The idea of writing a kata book got momentum when Peter said to me: "But a book is always a book. You have to write a book." This prompted me to apply for a grant and started this book project, which took quite a while. With his long-standing chief editor's background Peter gave me valuable advice on how to improve the text and helped with the photography. Staffan's extensive judo library provided much of the sources for this book. Thanks to his contribution, we were able to photograph at Hontai Judo dojo, where we built an excellent studio. Hannu Mustonen's great merit has been to ensure that the techniques are in line with the latest IJF international teachings.

Thanks also to my long-time judo friend Keijo Saarelainen (4th dan). Keijo was always ready to help and did a commendable job in acting as a filming assistant. For medical details I have been guided by Dr Juhani Vainio-Mattila (1st dan). The three of us are united by the Kotka Judo-club.

I would also like to thank all the judokas who acted as tori and uke. Mikko Tuominen, Samu Laitinen, Pasi Oinas, Mika Salsoila, Juha Turunen, Pekka Väyrynen, Kati Stoyanov-Pitkänen, Heli Vartiainen, Jussi Nikander and Otso Koski. The advanced technical quality in the book is thanks to their judo skills. In addition, they lasted the sometimes lengthy photographing sessions without compromising the quality.

I was also fortunate to get help from the publishing professionals. My friend Timo Vesterinen, a photographer by profession, helped me to set up the studio and advised me on editing the photos.

I am also grateful for the assistance of Jaakko Hannula (4th dan), Kelly Palmer (6 th dan) and Peter Martin (7th dan) in refining the English language and terminology used in this book. Thank you for the help. Also thanks to Jukka Aalto, whose handwriting is the graphic design of the book.

This book would not have been possible without the grant from Finnfoto – the Organisation of Finnish Photographers for Peter and me, which enabled us to ensure the technical quality of the photos. I took most of the photographs of nage-no-kata by myself, while the katame-no-kata photos were taken together with Peter.

Special thanks to Wolfgang Dax-Romswinkel for all his support and comments in the technical details and for correspondence during the project. I also wish to express my gratitude to Kodokan Judo Institute for all the historical material I received.

GLOSSARY

ago-oshi	ju-no-kata 5th technique
ashi-garami	katame-no-kata last technique, knee lock
ashi-guruma	a leg throw
ashi-waza	foot throw technique group
atemi	strike or kick to the vulnerable points of the body
ayumi-ashi	alternate step walk
bujutsu	traditional Japanese armed and unarmed martial artst
chikama	a distance of about 30 cm from uke
Dai Nippon Butoku Kai	the umbrella organisation for traditional Japanese martial arts
de-ashi-harai	foot and leg throws
Fukuda Hachinosuke	Fukuda was Kano's first jujutsu teacher (1828-1879)
garami	to entangle, tie. Also appears in the form karami
go	five
gō	hard
gokyo-no-waza	Kodokan's list of five technique classes
gō-no-kata	kata, which uses force first and then relaxes. Does not include throwing.
goshi	see koshi
gyaku-juji-jime	reverse cross-strangle
hadaka	bare, naked
hadaka-jime	bare-handed strangle of the trachea
hane-goshi	hip throw
harai-goshi	hip throw
hidari	left
hiki-te	pulling hand, usually on the sleeve
hiza	knee
hiza-guruma	a leg throw
hon-gesa-gatame	hold-down, controlling uke's shoulder
Iikubo Tsunetosi	Iikubo was Kano's kitō-ryū teacher (1835-1888)
IJF	International Judo Federation
Iso Masatomo	Iso was Kano's second tenjin shin'yō-ryū teacher (1818-1881)
itsutsu-no-kata	"kata of five" with five techniques
jigotai	defensive stance
jime	strangle, beginning the word with the form shime
joseki	place of honour, place of invitation, upper seat
joshi-goshinhō	women's self-defence kata
ju	perseverance, soft, ten
ju-no-kata	soft kata. In this kata, throws are not taken to the end

---

juji	cross
juji-gatame	arm lock on the straight arm between the legs
juji-jime-chokes	nami-, kata- and gyaku-juji-jime collective name
jujutsu	an old samurai form of hand-to-hand combat
kake	the throwing phase
kami-shiho-gatame	hold-down from the side of the head
kamiza	raised part of dojo, place of honour
Kano Jigoro	(1860-1938) The founder of Judo
kansetsu-waza	group of locking techniques. Can be performed on the mat or standing
kata	In Japanese, there are many characters that are read kata. It is a form, pattern, a formal series of movements (形 nage-no-kata) or shoulder (肩 kata-guruma, kata-gatame) or unilateral or bilateral (片, kata-juji-jime, kataha-jime) or way (方 kumi-kata).
kata-gatame	a hold-down in which uke's shoulder is controlled
kata-guruma	a hand throw
kataha-jime	a rear choke with one hand on the lapel
kata-juji-jime	cross-body choke with the palms facing to different directions
kata-juji-shibori-dori	a choke technique of tenjin shin'yō-ryū
kata-mawashi	ju-no-kata 4th technique
katame	to hold, to control
katame-no-kata	kata of techniques done on the mat
katame-waza	control techniques
kata-nokori	pre-dating randori, a form of training in jujutsu schools
kenka-yotsu	opposing holds. The opposite of ai-yotsu, which is a similar grip
kesa	Buddhist monk's robe
kesa-gatame	a hold-down, in which uke's shoulder is controlled
kime-no-kata	an old self-defence kata, fighting kata
kitō-ryū	a style of jujutsu taught by Kano before the founding of judo
kōgi	presentation
ko-ryū	old bujutsu schools
ko-soto-gari	a foot throw
ko-daore	7th technique of koshiki-no-kata
Kodokan	Japanese Judo Institute. Judo's main centre and primary home
Kodokan goshin-jutsu	a modern self-defence kata
kodomo-no-kata	children's kata
koshi	hip
koshiki-no-kata	old kitō-ryū kata, adapted for judo by Kano
koshi-waza	hip throwing technique group
kurai-dori	see kyoshi
kuzure-kami-shiho-gatame	hold-down from the side of the head with tori at an angle to uke
kuzushi	breaking one's balance
kyoshi	high kneeling position. In katame-no-kata, the right knee is up
mae-geri	straight kick forward with the ball of the foot

mae-ukemi	ukemi forward, with uke's stomach facing the mat
ma-sutemi-waza	sacrifice throw technique group with tori ending up on his back
migi	right
Mifune Kyuzo	one of Kano's students and 10th dan (1883-1965)
mondo	debate
nage-no-kata	15-technique throwing kata
nage-waza	throwing techniques
nami	common, ordinary
nami-juji-jime	a strangle with palms facing uke
nokori-ai	a form of training in jujutsu schools that preceded randori
o-goshi	a hip throw
o-guruma	a leg throw
okuri-ashi-harai	a foot throw
okuri-eri-jime	a rear choke with a grip on both lapels
omote	the outwardly visible part of the kata
osaekomi-waza	group of hold-down techniques
o-soto-gari	a foot throw
randori	take freedom, judo free practice
randori-no-kata	is a general term used to describe nage-no-kata and katame-no-kata.
randori technique	the throwing technique used in randor
reiho	greeting ceremony
riai	harmony of principles
Saigo Shiro	Kano's student and one of the 'gatekeepers of the Kodokan', (1866-1922)
sambo	Russian martial art inspired by judo, among others
sankaku-jime	triangle choke with the feet
sasae-tsurikomi-ashi	a foot throw
seiryoku-zen'yo-kokumin-taiiku	kata of the correct use of energy
seoi-nage	a hand throw
shiai	match, competition
shikko	knee movement in katame-no-kata
shime	strangle, spelled "jime" in the middle or at the end of a word
shime-waza	group of strangle techniques
Shimotomizaka	Kodokan's early training dojo
shizen-hontai	natural posture
shizentai	natural standing posture
shomen	place of honour at the front of the dojo
sode-tsurikomi-goshi	a hip throw
sukui-nage	a hand throw
sumi-gaeshi	a backward sacrifice throw
sumi-otoshi	a hand throw
suri-ashi	a movement where the feet stay close to the tatami

sutemi-waza	the technique group of sacrifice throws
tai-sabaki	body movement, turning
tandoku-renshu	training alone
tani-otoshi	a sacrifice throw on one's side
tenjin shin'yō-ryū	the jujutsu style first practised by Kano
tento	top of the head
te-waza	hand throwing technique group
toma	distance of about 1,2 m
tomoe-nage	a backward sacrifice throw
tori	the one who does the technique
tsugi-age	ju-no-kata 13th technique. It is also in the kime-no-kata
tsugi-ashi	a form of sliding step where the feet do not pass each other
tsukkake	in kime-no-kata 2nd and 11th techniques. Also found in Kodokan goshin-jutsu
tsukuri	preparation for the throw and tori's positioning for the throw
tsurikomi-goshi	a hip throw
tsuri-otoshi	an old sacrifice throw on the back. No precise information exists
tsuri-te	lifting hand, usually on the lapel
uchi-komi	repetition exercise
uchi-mata	a leg throw, of which there is also a hip throw version
ude-garami	an arm lock in which the hands are entangled around uke's hand
ude-gatame	direct arm lock with a control also with the neck
ude-hishigi	hand-breaking
uke	the person on whom the technique is applied
ukemi	fall
uki-goshi	a hip throw
uki-otoshi	a hand throw
uki-waza	a sacrifice throw on one's side
ura	the inner, hidden part of the kata
ura-nage	a backward sacrifice throw
waza	technique
Yamashita Yoshitsugu	Kano's student and one of the "Gatekeepers of the Kodokan", 10th dan (1865-1935)
yoko-gake	a sacrifice throw on one's side
yoko-guruma	a sacrifice throw on one's side
yoko-shiho-gatame	a hold-down from uke's side
yoko-sutemi-waza	a technique group for sacrifice throws with tori ending up on his side
yoko-tsuki	kime-no-kata 8th technique
Yokoyama Sakujiro	Kano's student and one of the 'Gatekeepers of Kodokan' (1864-1912)
zanshin	attentiveness after performance

BIBLIOGRAPHY

PRINTED SOURCES

DAIGO, TOSHIRO: *Wurftechniken des Kodokan Judo parts 1 - 3,* DJB Service GmbH, Frankfurt, 2018–2019

DEMACRO MA, SEVERAL AUTHORS, *Judo Kata, Practice, Competition, Purpose,* Via Media Publishing Company 2016

GÖRTZ, VOLKER UND GÜNTER, JÖRG: *Nage-no-kata,* Weinmann Berlin, 1990

HOARE, SYD: *The A–Z of Judo,* Ippon Books Ltd., Bristol 1994 (2006)

JENSEN, MAX: *Judo, valkoisesta mustaan vyöhön (from white to black belt),* Tammi, Helsinki 1985

KANO, JIGORO: *Kodokan Judo,* Kodansa USA Inc 2013

KAWAISHI, MIKONOSUKE: *The Seven Katas of Judo,* Foulsham& CO. Ltd, London 1957

KEIDEL, SVEN& BERNREUTHER, STEFAN: *Nage-no-kata lehren und lernen,* Meyer&Meyer, 2013

KICHISABURO, SASAKI: *Djudo a Japan Dzsiu-Dzsicu,* Budapest, 1907

KODOKAN KATA TEXT BOOK: *Nage-no-kata, katame-no-kata and kime-no-kata*

KORPIOLA, KYÖSTI AND TIMO: *Judo, Tie mustaan vyöhön, (Road to black belt),* Tammi, Latvia, 2010

KORPIOLA, TIMO: *Judo, Tie mestariksi (Road to Champion),* Bonum ltd Oy, Porvoo, 2014

LEGGETT, T. P.: *Kata Judo,* Foulsham& CO. Ltd, Hong Kong 1982

LE MÉE, PATRICK: *Le Randori No Kata,* Chiron, 2006

OTAKI, TAOKI & DRAEGER, DONN: *Judo, Formal Techniques,* Tuttle Publishing, Singapore, 1983

PASSION JUDO; SEVERAL AUTHORS: *Katas et jujitsu du 1 er au 4e dan OPC edition,* 2004

PFEIFFER, UTE & BAUER, GÜNTHER: *Judo Nage no kata,* Meyer&Meyer Sport, 2008

VOLKMANN, PETER: *Katame-no-kata,* Weinmann Berlin, 1990

YERKOW, CHARLES: *Judo Katas,* Prentice Hall Inc, USA, 1965

ARTICLES AND WEB SOURCES

ABERNETHY IAIN: *The Dynamic Nature of Judo Kata* danit.fi/ judosanasto (vocabulary)

DAX-ROMSWINKEL, WOLFGANG: *Grundwissen der Geschichte des Kōdōkan-Jūdō in Japan*

HOARE, SYD: *Development of Judo Competition Rules: Lecture Bath University Aug 2005*

IJF Nage-no-Kata educative project 2022 https://nrw. edumaps.de/104625/3264/l9rnokx8il

LLŶR JONES: *The Kano society bulletin: Kuzushi, Tsukuri and Kake in Kodokan Judo*

MURATA, NAOKI: *International Budo Symposium 2008: Transitions within Kodokan Judo Etiquette*

WIKIPEDIA ARTICLE: *Kodokan–Totsuka_rivalry*

VIDEOS

Gilon Nicolas, Nage-no-kata history EJU 2020

Kodokan Teaching videos: Nage-no-kata and katame-no-kata

Kodokan kata clinics 2014–2018

Kodokan Summer courses 2015–2018 / 2018 Gordon Okamura

Youtube videos from the World Kata Championships 2013-2019

Nordic Kata Open kata seminars: Wolfgang Dax-Romswinkel 2016–2024

HISTORICAL

NAGAOKA–ISOGAI 1910-luku, NAGAOKA-MURAKAMI 1920s (?), HAL SHARP films

CORRESPONDENCE

WOLFGANG DAX-ROMSWINKEL, FRANZ EDLINGER, TETSUJI SATO, MATHIAS HUNTZIGER

Mika Salsoila, Pasi Oinas, Keijo Saarelainen and Staffan Lindgren (above).

Peter Mickelsson, Samu Laitinen, Hannu Mustonen, Mikko Tuominen and Staffan Lindgren (below).

Hannu Mustonen, Peter Mickelsson, Samu Laitinen
and Mikko Tuominen (above).

Otso Koski, Pekka Väyrynen, Jorma Paasi and
Keijo Saarelainen (below).

The editorial board : Hannu Mustonen, Staffan Lindgren, Peter Mickelsson and Jorma Paasi (above).
Below also, Keijo Saarelainen, Mikko Tuominen, Samu Laitinen, Juha Turunen and Pekka Väyrynen.